The Evil God of Love

*A Definitive Answer to the
Ultimate Question*

Philip Joel Walls

ISBN: 979-8-9882956-7-9
ISBN (eBook): 979-8-9882956-6-2

To Jonathan

Keep the faith. There is zero evidence for atheism while an
abundance of evidence exists for the truth in Christ.

He Is Risen

Contents

Introduction

In the preface to his book, *The Problem of Pain*, C.S. Lewis admitted that he never intended to use his real name when publishing such literature. The content was, as he felt, of such a magnitude that he deemed himself unworthy of its authorship. It was Lewis' publicist who later ensured him the Christian world would not accept such literature unless it were in fact coming from a man of Lewis' continuing stature. Eventually, Lewis caved and poured out on paper so complex a book that precious few have ever come to grasp its true meaning or insight. As profound as Lewis' sentiments were, the reader is left with many unanswered questions. This book, *The Evil God of Love*, seeks to answer those questions.

By no means does this writer compare himself to Lewis, yet, he does presuppose the Christian world will likewise not accept the latter chapters of *this* book. Regardless, I did not publish these pages solely in hopes of persuading modern Christians to forfeit their estranged doctrines. The greater intention here is to provoke the atheist to a new way of understanding the ultimate question.

Lewis was a very rare breed of believer — a former atheist converted to Christianity, uniquely a result of his own contemplation toward the mysterious will and Holy Spirit of God, the only entity with the ability to compel a person to make such a profane statement as to suggest God not only *allows* suffering but in fact *requires* it as a means for understanding His purposes, our spiritual potential, and, indeed, our long forgotten angelic origins.

> But pain insists upon being attended to. God whispers to us in our pleasures, speaks in our conscience, but shouts in our pain: it is His megaphone to rouse a deaf world. [1]

My prayer is for this book to help men and women who can in any way relate to the atheist, C.S. Lewis, who, by struggling so thoroughly within his own consciousness, could not resist the urge to take the initial leap of faith and believe in a loving creator.

~

Among the most important questions presented by the atheist worldview, there exists a few questions above all others for which we Christians have failed to sufficiently answer. This book *is* that answer.

If the God of the Old Testament is the same God of the New Testament, how do we explain the clear discrepancies in His teachings?

If our God is a God of love, why do unthinkable tragedies befall innocent people?

If this "God of love" is the creator of all things and He truly does possess foreknowledge and sovereignty over His creation, why does He Himself perform such evil atrocities according to His own written testament? (Genesis 6–8; Genesis 18–19; Exodus 11–12; Leviticus 18:24–25; Numbers 21:2–3; Deuteronomy 9:3; 20:17; Joshua 6:17, 21; 1 Samuel 15)

Is God a hypocrite?

The default defensive posture of atheists will always precede a logical conversation with questions similar to these. How does a loving God command the death of entire nations of people in the Old Testament (which is tantamount to genocide) only to execute a complete 180 in His actions by commanding His followers to love one another and forgive their enemies in the New Testament? If our creator God is a God of forgiving love, *why* did He command the death of so many people?

This ideology is only one of the many grievances held by those who reject the Christian faith — or reject the existence of a "loving God" altogether. As often is the case, their reasoning behind posing such questions is subjective, not objective.

Many philosophers, poets, writers, and even kings and priests, both religious and atheistic, have attempted to address these dilemmas by postulating for and against the existence of an omnipotent loving creator. Yet, those who have contributed to the vast body of literature appear to be asking all the wrong questions. Said postulating suggests only a philosophical response concerning the *why's* of evil:

Why does evil exist?

Why did God create the potential for evil?

Why does God allow good, innocent people to suffer, even partaking in causing others to suffer by His own hand?

Who exactly is this *Evil God of Love*?

We will leave the unanswerable question of "why" to the philosophers. The question of *why* is and always has been a loaded question. What this author seeks to answer is the potential of *how*.

How did evil enter into existence? This is the correct question to ask. To suggest the question of "why does evil exist?" is a wickedly misleading presumption that creates the presupposition that God did in fact *intentionally* create evil. So *why* is there not more emphasis on the *who, what, where, when,* and *how*? These are all important questions as well.

We know God *allows* suffering to exist. The Christian testament states God Himself allowed His own begotten son to be tortured, publicly humiliated, and excruciatingly executed at the hands of evil men who had grown to hate Him. God allowed His own self-existence to be born into the flesh to experience persecution, torture, and evil, under the authoritarian hand of the enemy. But *why*? *Why* would God *allow* this?

If God has foreknowledge, *why* did He continue moving forward with creation knowing full well that He would later need to die by the hand of His own evil creation? Why go through all the trouble?

If God has foreknowledge, *why* did He create free will knowing in advance that free will would inevitably lead to rebellion and the need to "send a person to hell's fire"?

Again, the question is not *why*. It is *how*. The only way to answer the many questions listed herein is to ask the questions no Christian dares ask: *how* does evil exist?

Here is the ultimate question: did God knowingly and willingly create "people" He knew He would need to torture for all eternity? Is God really that cruel?

Is it God's desire that evil should exist, even knowing from before time began that His creation would eventually need to be punished? Or, is God only *allowing* this evil force, which He had no part in creating, to fully run its course to prove how patient and loving He truly is?

Furthermore, if God is the origin of evil, where does *love* come from? Why would an evil God create the capacity for *love*?

> But thou, O Lord, art a God full of compassion, and gracious, longsuffering, and plenteous in mercy and truth. (Psalm 86:15)

> The Lord is not slack concerning his promise, as some men count slackness; but is longsuffering to us-ward, not willing that any should perish, but that all should come to repentance. (2 Peter 3:9)

If the reader possesses the courage and wisdom to continue reading, they will come to understand that God did not create evil; Satan did. It is *us*, by the knowledge Satan passed down, who conjure up evil thoughts in our hearts to do the will of Satan — the creator of evil. We then act on those thoughts of evil (created by Satan), or we act on our thoughts of love (created by God), to bring them into existence.

The desire of *our* Loving Creator is that we deny he who created evil, which is of course "the dragon, that old serpent, which is the Devil, and Satan" (Revelation 20:2), and choose to do what is right, loving, and virtuous. Those who continue to practice Satan's knowledge knowing beyond the shadow of a doubt that God is a God of Love, and that Satan *is* the origin of all evil deeds, it is these souls whom God has promised will be punished for their wickedness.

~

This book will provide *four solutions* to answer the ultimate question: why does evil exist? The first solution presented is biblical, proving it was not God who created evil but Satan who summoned its treachery from before creation began. Such an understanding was previously covered in the chapter "What is the Matrix?" in the first book of this series, *The Christian Doctrine Paradox.* [2] By expounding upon this biblical teaching once again, we will uncover *how* evil first came into existence.

The other three solutions are a simple, logical response as to *how* evil may have occurred in the first place. Though we will dabble in the "why's" throughout this book, this is not a class in philosophy. This is, in itself, the most basic definition of how evil could have entered God's existence while God simultaneously maintains His absolute sovereignty and pure love.

If you search, you will find the question of "how" has never firmly been addressed. Our Christian philosophers have only ever bothered with the "why" of evil.

They will teach, *Why? Because God said so, that's why. And He will do all His goodwill and pleasure.* Believers make these claims quoting passages such as Daniel 4, Isaiah 46, and others.

> All the peoples of the earth are regarded as nothing. He does as he pleases with the powers of heaven and the peoples of the earth. No one can hold back his hand or say to him: "What have you done?" (Daniel 4:35; NIV)

> Declaring the end from the beginning, and from ancient times the things that are not yet done, saying, My counsel shall stand, and I will do all my pleasure. (Isaiah 46:10)

One notable example among many is John MacArthur's position regarding "The Problem of Evil," [3] to which the atheists, such as Richard Dawkins, respond without hesitation:

> The God of the Old Testament is arguably the most unpleasant character in all fiction: jealous and proud of it; a petty, unjust, unforgiving control-freak; a vindictive, bloodthirsty ethnic cleanser; a misogynistic, homophobic, racist, infanticidal, genocidal, filicidal, pestilential, megalomaniacal, sadomasochistic, capriciously malevolent bully. [4]

Dawkins' view of God can be proven in error by addressing the *how* in place of the *why*.

The problem with this, as you will see, is that Christians will undoubtedly reject answers to these questions for one simple reason. The latter three solutions mentioned in this book cannot be categorically proven with scripture. Even so, we should note the duality in this type of reasoning. The burden of proof does not necessarily fall on those who cannot prove such a teaching with scripture, but equally so to those who cannot *dis*prove such teachings with scripture. Some will argue this statement creates a logical fallacy. However, given evidence for the duality complex, it can be proven the logical fallacy is also a two-way street. Both the burden of proof and the logical fallacy argument(s) are at the same time both true and false, for both sides of the debate, creating a paradox that cannot be resolved outside the order of *faith*. A Christian believer can no more *disprove* the theories written in this book than an atheist can *prove* the nonexistence of God. Hence, the paradox emerges.

In Chapter 1, we cover historical sources and their baseline conclusions for the problem of evil. Chapter 2 is suggested evidence on how the burden of proof and logical fallacies are a two-way street. Often, Christians are thrown under the bus when suggesting the burden of proof is on us. To suggest that should be the case is overtly bias and unrealistic. In Chapter 3 we revisit the Matrix chapter from the previous book in this series to clarify a few points leading to the topic of evil. Chapter 4 is a proposed depiction of how Satan and God did not originate in the same realm, or dimension. Evidence is cited and many claims are made to which the Christian world will likely have this author stoned for heresy (a touch of hyperbole was used for dramatic effect but is not outside the *realm* of possibility; pun intended). In Chapters 5 and 6, we discuss the potential origins of both foreknowledge and free will, the two most important, and at the same time misleading, topics concerning the problem of evil. Finally, in Chapter 7, additional information of various sorts is proposed to both the believer and nonbeliever.

Heresy? Blasphemy? Call it what you want. Nevertheless, this book offers solid evidence for answers that will likely warrant new conversations that have never been had.

If a person were to offer potential answers to a question that has never been sufficiently answered and to answer said question with a logical view to which even the most devout atheist would be required to rethink their position, wouldn't it be worthwhile to have that conversation? Why should these answers be silenced by the Christian community calling it heresy, or worse, if it does not dismiss God's sovereignty nor His authority to execute judgment over a fallen creation?

> But sanctify the Lord God in your hearts: and *be ready always to give an answer to every man that asketh you a reason of the hope that is in you...*" (1 Peter 3:15)

If an atheist were to publicly confront you with the question, "Why is your God so damned evil?" How would *you* respond? **[5]**

CHAPTER 1

Historical Sources Address "The Problem of Evil"

The many historical sources to comment on the subject of evil are all asking the wrong questions. As a result of these misleading philosophical assumptions, we have all come to an unfortunate stalemate in a game of chess, that is, "the ultimate question." The book you are now reading will put the atheist in check. When the last page is turned and the cover is closed, it will be their move once again. Truth be told, neither side will ever have the ability to finish the game. It is only the King who possesses the insight to declare checkmate (Revelation 19:16).

In one way or another, every human soul has at some point asked himself or herself this same question: why (*fill in the blank*)? The atheist might ask, if a loving God truly does exist, *why* are humans required to deal with so much pain and suffering? The agnostic might ask, *why* should I cling to religion when religion is the source of so much death and warfare throughout history? Why bother? There is no way to prove God exists one way or the other. The Christian of course will state plainly that God is a God of Love and we do not have the authority to question His judgment. Nevertheless, this thinking has not deterred countless atheists, philosophers, and religious zealots across the planet from questioning God's motives.

It should go without saying that we Christians cannot speak for all atheists worldwide, but for the prominent atheists who have chosen to write on the subject of evil, we have a great deal of insight into their ideology. They tell us *the Holy Bible* should *not* be trusted as a historical document. They claim it is either a work of fiction or an altered set of historical events filled with people, places, and outlandish miracles that cannot be proven. That, or it is an even grander conspiracy to keep the subject populations in check.

Imagine if the smartest and richest people throughout history devised a brilliant plan to rule over the poor, less fortunate, less intelligent people. Their board of directors would say something to the effect of, "Let us tell the people, an all-powerful God has given us the authority to rule over them...and He will punish them if they disobey their masters... yes, let us also say, they will all be sent to hells fire for all eternity for disobeying this creed...if we can get them to believe such things, we will have the perfect opportunity to keep ourselves in power."

The above statement is not entirely fiction. It exists both in the mind of atheists, as well as our world leaders and ruling elite. All of whom either outright reject a Loving Creator

God or falsify God's presence in their lives by "playing the part" of a religious person as some form a PR stunt or political objective.

No matter what religion a person ascribes to, the so-called problem of evil has never been sufficiently addressed — certainly, not by the Christian worldview. The unspoken creed of addressing evil for Christians has always been "repent and join the church, or burn in hell!"

"But *why* is this the case?" The skeptics will ask, "Why will I be sent to hell for an evil preordained by my supposedly loving creator?"

The problem of evil was first introduced as far back as the Babylonian epic of creation, *Enuma Elish,* and the *Epic of Gilgamesh* originating from ancient Mesopotamia. In both of these legendary tales, the reader is presented with the most fundamental human reflex of evil, which is of course to *look up* and blame an outside force. In such tales, we are directed to imagine a cosmic battle of good versus evil taking place in the heavenly realms. We mere mortals are nothing more than casualties of a war-torn cosmos with no end in sight, that is, no favorable end from what little information the gods allow us to possess.

Later, during the era of the Greek philosophers Socrates, Plato, and Aristotle, all contemporaries and successors of one another, we begin to see a new way of understanding evil emerge. Plato was a disciple of Socrates where the two of them grew together in knowledge. As time went on, Plato took under his wing the well-known Aristotle. The evolution of thought between these three characters ultimately led to Aristotle producing his own matured view. That being, the problem of evil boils down to a "lack of will power" to follow one's own inherent good nature. In essence, if every action we humans took part in were to be ruled by a wholesome moral compass, there would be no evil to combat and, therefore, no question of "why" evil exists.

As time would pass, the theologians and religious types would continue to seek answers to the problem of evil from a religious perspective, and not that of a secular philosophical one.

Dante Alighieri wrote a poem that is said to have shaped the Christian perception of hell quite possibly more than any other work in history. In it, he offers a dire warning posted on a sign directly above the gates of hades:

> Through me one goes into the town of woe,
> through me one goes into eternal pain,
> through me among the people that are lost.
>   Justice inspired my high exalted Maker;
>   I was created by the Might divine,
>   the highest Wisdom and the primal Love.
> Before me there was naught created, save
> eternal things, and I eternal last;
> all hope abandon, ye that enter here! [6]

Dante does not answer the question of "why" in his dark yet brilliant poem. He only states emphatically that hell exists as a destination for the wicked.

The Reformation is known to be a turning point in the way people were thinking about Christianity, heaven, and hell. For the longest time, there were no real debates taking place on a broader scale until the Reformation in the sixteenth century and beyond. Martin Luther and John Calvin, notably, were the two philosophical and doctrinal giants of the era to offer an alternative to the status quo. They proposed the notion for the first time that we do not need the church hierarchy to be our intermediary between us and God, but rather, grace and forgiveness are offered by Christ, and not by the admission of a priest. These two men would essentially force the Christian world into a new way of understanding our faith. As with most great thinkers and theologians, understanding the concept of evil was a necessity.

Most notably for Luther was the idea that Satan is a powerful angelic figure who can tempt us into allowing evil to exist. That is to say, without Satan, we would not have evil in our lives, and evil would not exist. Calvin, on the other hand, did not share Luther's sentiments. One of the main contributions Calvin made on the subject was the total depravity of the human race and the idea of predestination—that because we are so depraved, we are somehow predestined to salvation in Jesus Christ or damnation in hell's fire.

> "In fact... the proper theological term for what Calvin believed in and affirmed is a super-lapsarian double predestination... What it means is that Calvin believes that the blessed are predestined to Heaven and the damned are predestined to Hell, and they are both predestined in those ways – that's a double predestination – from before the Fall: "Super lapsos," "before the lapse," "before the Fall".

Calvin thinks that before humans fell, God foreknew and preordained – not just knew but determined, ordered, willed – that some would be blessed and some would be damned." [7]

Niccolo Machiavelli was another prominent thinker to arise in the Reformation era, but certainly not to the advantage of Christian faith. Machiavelli believed not only in the *necessity* of evil, or "the right to be bad," but also in its insistence. As a secularist who did not share a faith in Christ but, more so, took the nihilists' approach to his philosophy, he essentially believed that politicians *must* be evil if they are to rule their subject populations effectively.

Another man by the name of Thomas Hobbes shared a similar ideology. Evil was not a spiritual battle that needs to be tended to, but more so a result of political maneuvering as a social construct. Hobbes saw the world through the lens of what life would look like without civilized society. Picture an Australian tribe of aborigines who do not take part in trade or commerce, politics, education, or social norms of any kind. Now compare this to a civilized society such as Rome during the Reformation. Evil would exist in an entirely different context by following a political structure of what is deemed acceptable in that place and time. A distant tribe of aborigines however would have their own definition of "evil." Perhaps for the aborigine, evil would be stealing a family's food that they had hunted or gathered personally. In Rome, this act of stealing food would simply be a "crime" with not too harsh a punishment attached. In the outback, however, it is pure evil to take another man's food — his livelihood, his ability to eat and live. Therefore, as Hobbes suggests, evil is a construct of society believing that *we* create what is evil and what is not.

The concept of God creating evil comes into play once again in the essays of Michel de Montaigne. Montaigne believed in the idea that the religions "zealots" are the sole cause of evil in the world. This is a similar belief shared by the atheists of our modern era. How many times have nations and ideologies gone to war over their religious beliefs? God only knows. How many times has a nation been attacked as a result of a religious belief? This question is a difficult subject for the believer to refute because the question is addressing a known evil — war in the name of God. If only there were no God, and therefore no religion, we would all be living a blissful existence of harmony… right?

In total contrast to Montaigne are the writings of Blaise Pascal. Zealots are not to blame in Pascal's mind. Those who take the blame are the people who do not take their religious beliefs seriously enough. If all the world were to love God as Christ commands, there would be no evil. Pascal disagreed with Montaigne wholeheartedly by defending the Christian faith. If we were to follow Christ's teachings (love God and love one another), there would be no evil in the world, which is true. He believed that evil is not a result of God's creation, but a result of mankind not following God's commandments to express love to our fellowmen. Simply put, Montaigne believed God to be the cause of evil, while Pascal believed Satan to be its origin.

> ...Satan's sin is rebellion against God, but Satan sees his
> rebellion as prompted by God and is unwilling to own up
> to his responsibility. Interestingly, the poem depicts Satan
> as a master of possibilities, of hypotheticals, but never able
> to settle on any of them. **[8]**

The above excerpt from *Why Evil Exists* is a synopsis of *Paradise Lost*, a poem written by John Milton in the seventeenth century. It is known to be one of the most "epic" poems of all time concerning the topic of evil and is only rivaled in its greatness by the infamous Dante's Inferno. For Milton, the idea of God's creation, in this case Satan, rebelling against his creator is ever-present. This type of thinking does not stray from the "why" of evil's existence. It is a fair question: *why* did God knowingly create Satan?

In the mind of Gottfried Wilhelm Leibniz, however, God created "the most perfect world He possibly could have," given the inevitable circumstances of free will. His assumption as a prominent mathematician and scientist as well as being the most influential philosopher of his day was to suggest that this creation is as good as it gets. He asserts that the universe we occupy is the best possible outcome of a good-willed God. In Leibniz' view, there exists a belief similar (yet overtly contradictory) to the proposal laid out in Chapter 5 of *this* book. Before God began creating (whoever God is), His intentions were nothing less than perfectly good-natured. After creation had gotten underway, God would have at some point in time noticed the possibility of imperfection. When this thought first occurred to God, He decided it would be prudent to "do the best He can" with what He had started. This of course reduces God's perfect foreknowledge to a lesser value of the ability to "make a mistake." A possibility that we as Christians are trained to believe is utterly incomprehensible. It should be noted that Genesis 6:6 places such a theology in jeopardy.

A few modern philosophers have claimed Immanuel Kant is the most revolutionary thinker to ever tackle this subject. Where his contemporaries were focused on evil being an outside force that we must somehow grasp and overcome, he focuses on the idea of evil being a reaction from us, the acting subject. Until this time, people were focused on the outside force (presumably Satan) when Kant essentially believed the force is not external, but internal. His publications, the *Critique of Pure Reason* and *Religion within the Bounds of Bare Reason*, are attempts to appeal to the rational logic that all humans possess, or, as he refers to it, "reason." Kant reasoned with the need to understand why religion develops the way it does, as opposed to focusing on the specifics of one religion or the other. In doing so, the "morality" of humans is a result of logic and reason, and not a specific religious belief.

> Kant pioneered a method known as "demythologizing," in which the resolution to a problem we face is recognized to go beyond mere cognition to an appreciation of the power and wisdom of myth. ...Myth (religion) has a profundity of meaning and a density of symbolic reference beyond the ability of any philosophical system to fully articulate. [9]

The need to escape this "myth" of religious tradition and focus on logical thought, or "reason," is the primary role he played in this conversation, once again, essentially taking God out of the equation, which in fact is required if we are to understand evil in its proper context.

We would be remiss if we skipped this next individual due to his direct relevance to evil in our current world.

Karl Marx asserted the only "evil" in the world was to segregate the masses by class, social status, or financial gain. And the only way to eradicate the existence of this evil is to take from the "have's" and give to the "have not's." Or rather, force those who have independently acquired large sums of money to give that money to the poor. In the mind of Karl Marx, the only way to eradicate evil was to allow the government to "fairly" distribute money as if money is the source of happiness, or the antithesis of evil. He believed that if everyone were on the same financial playing field, people would have no need to be angry with a different class of human, and a peaceful coexistence would ensue. Let us not forget that Marx believed in the "evolution" of races and societies. This type of ideology not only dismisses the existence of God, but further denies Christ's teaching that essentially says the same thing (give to the poor) yet in a completely different context.

Christ commands His followers to help one another—to give to the poor *willingly*, making all things equal so that no person can hold their personal wealth or power of influence over another person. It is quite evident when reading through the gospel message that following Christ's commandments did in fact produce an absence of evil, for a time. Once Christ's teachings were corrupted by false doctrine, the evil that had begun to flee the heart of the believer was once again showing up in droves.

Communism is to have the *state* forcefully take money from the wealthy independent creators and give it to the less prominent masses. This ideology assumes that the intermediary will remain pure at heart, not allowing the money passing through their hands to corrupt their conscience. In the case of every attempted communist regime planet earth has ever known, this is clearly not the case. The bulk of the money *never* makes its way into the hands of poor people. The money is *not* distributed fairly. If Karl Mark were the man to mediate the taking and giving of money, are we to assume Mr. Marx would always be honest enough to distribute the money fairly? Communism is putting our faith in man to solve the ills of evil, while Christianity (freely giving to those in need) takes the intermediary — the potential for corruption — out of the equation. Without the intermediary managing the finances and distribution of wealth (communism), we would be free to help each other as everyone has need (the Kingdom of God). Communism (the ideology of Marx and his elite companions) is Satan's version of God's kingdom, a kingdom where everyone freely gives to those in need, where no man, woman, or child will ever be found lacking, in turn, ridding ourselves of evil by loving one another as Christ commands.

Communism, and the entire ideology Marx proposed, is pure evil. Perhaps Marx and his close associates were well schooled in the teachings of Machiavelli. A little "controlled evil" has the potential to go a long way and is necessary to successfully control the masses. As true as that appears to be, it does not answer the question of *who, what, where, when,* and *how* did evil originate?

Nietzsche, Dostoevsky, Conrad, Freud, Camus, Arendt— these are all prominent and notable figures that could fill the pages of countless books, but to what end? Nobody has ever attempted to ask the question of *how.* Are we so caught up in our wondering philosophies of "why" that we cannot propose a more logical and even more obvious alternative?

~

Even with all the opposition listed above, true Christians continue to plead their case after ages of persecution delivered by the hands of those who hate us. We believe Jesus is who He said He is: *the creator of heaven and earth* (John 1). This is the most important aspect of our belief and should be firmly planted in the hearts and minds of the skeptics if for nothing more than an accurate understanding of who we are as Christians. The reason we place our faith in Christ is due to the resurrection. We believe He is literally co-creator and equal in deity with the Almighty God because He is the only historical figure who claimed to be exactly that while also showing Himself alive after His death and leaving an overwhelming abundance of evidence to prove the case! [10] This is undoubtedly why C.S. Lewis, after having searched his heart, could not refrain from asking God, *I believe you now… but why Lord?*

The reason prominent atheists such as Dawkins, Carlin, and others cannot understand God's judgment is that they cannot understand God's parables. They lack the courage and wisdom to do as C.S. Lewis did and at least *try* to understand the will of God, which, by the way, is why they refuse to open their ears or soften their hearts. They have no desire to believe or seek the truth and no capacity whatsoever to allow their hearts to be ruled by an outside force. Stubbornness and pride reign in their consciousness, which have, in turn, led to their desire to create their own gods by *becoming* their own gods. This is exactly what happened in the Garden of Eden. Satan convinced "Eve" that by rejecting the will of God she could "become like God" (Genesis 3:5).

> For this people's heart is waxed gross, and their ears are dull of hearing, and their eyes they have closed; lest at any time they should see with their eyes, and hear with their ears, and should understand with their heart, and should be converted, and I should heal them. (Matthew 13:15)

> And for this cause God shall send them strong delusion, that they should believe a lie: [12]That they all might be damned who believed not the truth, but had pleasure in unrighteousness. (2 Thessalonians 2:11–12)

It truly is this simple. If the unbeliever were to take that initial leap of faith, the way C.S. Lewis had, their hard hearts would be softened, and their marked foreheads would be sealed by God. They would be healed from this cancerous question of "why."

As Peter Kreeft suggests in his *Fundamentals of the Faith* [11], this one question has caused more disbelief than any other question in history.

> More People have abandoned their faith because of the problem of evil than for any other reason. It is certainly the greatest test of faith, the greatest temptation to unbelief. And it's not just an intellectual objection. We feel it. We live it. That's why the book of Job is so arresting … The unbeliever who asks that question is usually feeling resentment toward and rebellion against God, not just lacking evidence for his existence. C.S. Lewis recalls that as an atheist he "did not believe God existed. I was also very angry with him for not existing. I was also angry with him for having created the world." [12]

Though Kreeft makes several invaluable and logical points, he, like many others, is still not addressing the crucial question of *how*. He essentially stated God's position as, *"My dearly beloved children. I feel your pain. To prove how sorry I am for creating evil, I am going to crucify my son,"* once again taking the "how" it happened out of the equation.

> The Father's love sent his Son to die for us to defeat the power of evil in human nature: that's the heart of the Christian story. We do not worship a deistic God, an absentee landlord who ignores his slum; we worship a garbageman God who came right down into our worst garbage to clean it up. How do we get God off the hook

for allowing evil? God is not off the hook; God is the hook. That is the point of the crucifix. **[13]**

A more recent contributor to this topic is Greg Welty in his book *Why Is There Evil In The World (And So Much Of It)?* **[14]** Welty's main argument as mentioned in the introduction is to suggest we (the Christian) cannot use anything other than the Bible when attempting to assimilate skeptics into the Christian faith. He offers two basic points to suggest this is the case:

> First, Christians are already committed to the entire truth of the Bible. They cannot run away from its teaching about God, the world, and God's relation to it. It would be foolish for Christians to hide the teachings of the bible from those who are skeptical about the truth of the Christian faith, in order to ultimately persuade them to embrace the teachings of the Bible.
>
> ...Second, having studied the problem of evil as a philosopher of religion for quite a few years, it seems to me that the best philosophical reasoning available on the subject helps to confirm what Christians already claim to know on the basis of the Bible. So the role of philosophy can be to complement and confirm the Christian message. Such reasoning, though not found in the bible, can be used to defend the biblical teaching from various spurious objections, by clarifying what the alternatives really are, and *by bringing to light unwarranted assumptions* that are often presented by critics as eminently reasonable but in reality are anything but that... **[15; emphasis mine]**

The final point made by Welty in his introduction was to suggest a thought similar to my own: the burden of proof does not solely rely on the believer but equally so to the skeptic. Yet we differ on the main topic at hand. This idea to part ways with the question of "why" has never been addressed by anyone, at least, none that is discoverable by *this* author in his many years of research.

> My main point throughout will be that although we as humans may not know enough to 'rule in' a theodicy as explaining a particular evil on a particular occasion, the burden of proof is on the critic of Christianity to show that we know enough to *rule out* the applicability of the available theodicies. In the very nature of the case I don't think this burden can be met, and so I don't think the 'problem of evil' can ever be an *intellectually rational* reason to reject the existence of God. [16]

One of the more thought-provoking books on this subject in recent years is a book titled *Is God a Moral Monster?* written by Paul Copan. This is a wonderful book to offer a person struggling with the "why" of scripture.

> God doesn't take more credit than he deserves. For example, he doesn't claim to make the choices that morally responsible humans must make, nor does he take credit for being the author of evil in the name of "sovereignty" (which some Christians tend to assign to him when they praise God *for* evil things). No, God doesn't "think more highly of himself than he ought to think" (Rom. 12.3) Rather, he thinks quite accurately about himself. [17]

For the atheist, naturally, this is not enough. It is never enough to bring forward yet another book written about the "why" of a very confusing series of Old Testament scriptures. Hence, the need to break the conversation wide open by addressing the question of "how."

~

How has no one ever thought to suggest that God is not to blame for the creation of evil? Why does the philosopher assume they need an explanation for "why" God created evil? Why do the atheists and even Christian believers never attempt to place the blame for evil on anyone other than God?

The root cause of this misrepresentation is that Satan was one of God's creations. Therefore, God created evil because God created Satan, right? And if God had foreknowledge from a time before creation began, He would have known Satan would turn out to be evil, right? The argument appears to have a solid foundation. How do we the believers refute these statements?

What would you say if I told you this question is based on nothing more than false assumptions regarding creation, foreknowledge, and *free will*? Assumptions that can **not** be proven with standard biblical exegesis? These assumptions cannot be proven with the Bible! So, who is to say it is a sound Christian doctrine if the doctrine cannot be proven with the Bible?

Before we address these false assumptions, however, we need to first address the burden of proof and the many logical fallacies surrounding this topic.

CHAPTER 2

The Burden of Proof and Logical Fallacies

The atheist worldview demands the burden of proof must belong to the believer. They claim that *we* the believers must prove God's existence as well as disprove their own theories of origin. They are by no means approaching this debate objectively or rationally. For instance, here is a logical question to which the atheist cannot answer objectively.

How can a Christian convert an atheist who has already made their decision not to believe? The atheist can then respond, *I would ask you the same question, you hypocrite. Your mind is already made up, and you refuse to believe our scientific theory.*

The same atheists will tell us the universe and everything in it came into existence due to a "big bang" created from nothingness. They do so while claiming scientific *theory* as the springboard for their belief systems, once again placing the burden of proof on others by maintaining it is we the believer who have not yet *proven* the scientific theory in error. This is bias subjective reasoning. Not to mention, it is an ignorant lie. Numerous scientists have proven scientifically the facts that support the creationist view. The evidence for the Biblical version of creation is overwhelmingly abundant **[18] [19] [20] [21] [22]**. However, atheists (and even some Christian groups) emphatically refuse to hear this evidence while clinging to their own theories like a drowning man to a life preserver. Furthermore, there is zero scientific evidence to support evolution and the big bang, which of course is why they literally refer to it as a "theory."

In truth, the burden of proof is a double-edged sword. It is a razor-sharp blade cutting through the arguments of both the believer and nonbeliever. It is a coin with two sides that atheists refuse to admit exists. The burden of proof is a two-way street. Where the Christian has chosen to ride a bicycle, the atheist will object to using anything other than a helicopter to unfairly navigate the conversation.

The burden of proof is undoubtedly shared with the atheists for a few reasons.

First, atheism is a religious belief that cannot be proven with science. It requires faith to be an atheist.

Atheism claims absolutism, meaning, they are making a definitive statement of assurance which requires a very strong faith to emphatically believe (without evidence) that God does *not* exist and that everything in creation came from nothing. The nonexistence of a creator God cannot be proven. Identical to theism, atheism is not neutral from bias.

It is a statement of absolute value, that is, God does not exist. Period.

Agnosticism is much different. This ideology is only a philosophical presumption that states one cannot prove *or* disprove the existence of God and is therefore neutral from bias. Agnosticism is not an absolute value resembling a religious belief. Therefore, anything other than agnosticism claiming to be an absolute fact (God exists or God does *not* exist) must co-share the scientific burden of proof.

Second, atheism (a religious belief requiring faith) is being taught to children in public schools as if it were a scientific fact even though they (the atheists) have *zero* evidence to support their belief. All the while, the evidence for the Christian faith is plentiful **[10] [18] [19] [20] [21] [22]**, yet, the powers that be refuse to allow Christians to share their evidence for creation in those same public schools.

Another item we need to understand is how atheism, evolution, and the big bang theory have no separation in their ideologies. They are all part of the same thought process derived from how "we came from nothing" and yet we exist. Evolution, the big bang, and atheism all go hand in hand. Atheism, evolution, and the "big bang" are not science; they are a religious belief that offers the world no evidence of any kind whatsoever.

God does *not* exist (no evidence).

God *does* exist (there is evidence!).

Jesus Christ was a real historical figure **[10]** who claimed to be God and co-eternal as the creator, performed miracles, showed Himself alive after His death, and even informed

His followers that He has a plan to remove evil from existence once and for all.

~

To claim evolution, the big bang, and atheism are not fully interconnected is outright ignorance, or a flat-out lie. The Christian belief clearly states "God created," taking the chance of accidental, happenstantial creation out of the equation. Evolution cannot be proven with science any more than Jesus Christ raising a person from the dead and walking on water can be proven with science. Evolution is not a scientific principle; it is a religious belief with zero observable scientific evidence to back its claims—*exactly* like Jesus walking on water. The simple fact that atheists and evolutionists have a creation story (created from nothing, by no one) is undeniable evidence to prove their "theory" is a religion, their holy trinity being chaos, fake science, and disinformation.

We must admit however that as Christians, this should not be our greatest concern. We are *in* the world, but we are not *of* the world (John 15:19), and we should not worry ourselves with other religious ideologies, nor the governments of the world whom God Himself has granted authority to rule over us (Jeremiah 25:8–9; John 19:11; Mark 12:17; Romans 13:1–7; 1 Timothy 2:1–2; 1 Peter 2:18–20).

> Servants, be submissive to your masters with all respect, not only to those who are good and gentle, but also to those who are unreasonable. [19]For this finds favor, if for the sake of conscience toward God a person bears up under

sorrows when suffering unjustly. [20]For what credit is there if, when you sin and are harshly treated, you endure it with patience? But if when you do what is right and suffer for it you patiently endure it, this finds favor with God. (1 Peter 2:18–20; NAS)

Christ has called us to be His hands and feet while He is away preparing a new heaven and a new earth (Isaiah 65:17; Matthew 19:28; Acts 3:21; 2 Peter 3:7–11; Revelation 21–22). He left us with the commandment to practice peace, love, hope, and charity. Not least of all, He commanded us to speak the truth.

Unfortunately, what Peter stated in his letter to the church shown above is true. We will suffer unjustly for Christ's namesake. Those who hate Christ's message of love and repentance have forced Christian hands to cover their own mouths and much, much worse. It is far past time we accept our responsibilities as the persecuted, raise our hands to God, and speak out against their satanic lies.

~

Atheism is hypocrisy in its purest form. If they are going to demand their religion of evolution be taught in tax-payer-funded institutions, why are Christians prohibited from performing the same? Atheists are using tax dollars, collected from Christians, to preach their religion to *our* children. The burden of proof is now on them. Otherwise, Christians should not be forced to pay for the atheist religion to be taught to our children in public schools. The same way a private Christian school refuses to teach the fake science of the big bang, evolution, and transgenderism, the publicly taxpayer-funded schools refuse to teach children about our Loving Creator.

Consider the fact that Christian parents pay for their children to attend private schools (where their religious beliefs are being upheld) only when they have a child attending that school. At the same time, these same Christians are forced to pay taxes to the public schools (even if they do not have children attending those public schools). The Christian who chooses to attend a private school is paying out of pocket for both religions, atheism and Christianity.

On the other hand, atheists are not forced to pay for the Christian worldview. Christians are forbidden from teaching their religion, Jesus Christ is King and Creator, in public schools. While at the same time, atheists are *never forced*, as Christians are forced, to pay for a belief they believe to be in error.

If atheists want to teach their religion of fake science to children, they should open their own private institutions the same way we Christians are *forced* to do so. No money from the government should be granted...ever. We could then allow the free market to expose their attendance records as the abysmal failure it would no doubt become.

The above statements have been made for the purpose of understanding the atheists unimaginably hypocritical religion of satanic fake science. The atheists teach their religion in public schools, and they do so at the taxpayers' expense. Hence, the burden of proof is now on them or, at least, should be shared, and they should publicly admit their own logical fallacies. This is not about taxes any more than it is about the burden of proof.

The truth is, we will likely never hear a confession from the devout nonbelievers. The earth we share is Satan's domain, for now (Ephesians 2:2; John 14:30; 2 Corinthians 4:4; James 4:4). These statements are not written to suggest those in charge of this world will ever alter their satanic philosophies or eradicate the corruption in their degenerate institutions but only to prove the forked-tongued, double-standard nature of the atheist's unproven and unsubstantiated religion.

~

More to the point of this book, the atheist religion will force Christians to address the "problem of Evil" while pointing their fingers at God (ironically, while claiming God does not exist). Yet, have they ever once raised their voices to speak out against the "problem of Love"? No, they have not.

As noted, this paradox has a mirror image. An equilibrium of sorts. A symmetry of opposite proportions. No matter how they choose to pose the question, there is always an opposite context. They are the yin to our yang, so to speak.

Think about this in terms of how the animal kingdom interacts with animals from different species. In the animal kingdom, there is no single species going out of its way to feed another species. The lion does need feed the gazelle out of the kindness of its heart. It will kill the gazelle to nourish its own tribe. This is the same "survival of the fittest" taught in human evolution. The atheist believes we are nothing more than animals. Albeit, animals who happen to be more evolved than the other species.

In the animal kingdom, there is no single species going out of their way to build a shelter for another species. The bear does not offer its den to the coyote, nor the snake offer its hibernaculum to the mouse. The bear will pummel the coyote for entering its lair, and the snake will feast on the mouse.

In the kingdom of mankind, however, despite the countless unimaginable tragedies to befall innocent people due to the existence of evil, these same innocent people will respond to pain and suffering with love and kindness, to illuminate the darkness, even when it is completely inconvenient to do so. If God is as evil as the atheists propose, where does this love come from?

When a person driving a long cold winter's road pulls over to help another stuck in the snow after so many other vehicles have passed, where does that help come from?

When a local church house pools resources to help the struggling family down the road put food in their pantries or shoes on their feet, even though that family does not "attend church," where does that generosity come from?

When a man allows another man's family to live on his land freely until that family is once again capable of getting a place of their own while knowing said man's family will likely never be able to repay him, where does that goodwill and charity come from?

These types of Christian virtues are only a few among many scenarios I have witnessed personally. Virtuous acts of kindness happen every day, all around the world, while *never* getting the attention they deserve.

You see, the atheist will put so much emphasis on how God allows so much pain, suffering, and evil, but never once do they mention the stories of goodwill, love, and charity that God also *allows* under the same earthly circumstances.

Why do people blame God for all the evil in the world yet refuse to cast upon God the guilt for all His love and kindness?

If God is *not* a God of love, where does this goodness, love, and charity come from? It is certainly not a result of evolution and self-preservation which is what "survival of the fittest" is teaching our children. Survival of the fittest, which is evil, belongs to evolution and atheism. Who is to blame for its opposite? Who is to blame for love, generosity, and compassion? Human nature? Certainly not.

A person I love once confessed to me that they believe Christians are hypocrites. A false Christian, yes. Christ Himself pointed out how many of these self-professed followers are in fact wolves disguised in sheep's clothing (Matthew 7:15). A true Christian however follows Christ's teachings and carries a love for their fellow brothers and sisters everywhere they go. A true Christian is the antithesis of hypocrisy.

When the banner of truth and objectivity has finally dawned in the atheist's heart, the inevitable conclusion will be obvious. True hypocrisy and ignorance are a product of the satanic religion known to this unbelieving world as atheism.

A faith in Christ as King and His teachings to love our fellowmen as He loves us presents a light to the world that no religion can offer. Atheism and evolution, on the other hand, have nothing to offer humanity other than that which is deduced from the animal kingdom. Self-preservation and survival of the fittest. And lest we forget their vile and unverifiable god of creation, fake science.

CHAPTER 3

The Matrix Revisited

It would be prudent to revisit *The Christian Doctrine Paradox* before diving into the last three aforementioned "definitive answers."

This is the first of "four solutions" mentioned in the introduction.

If you have not already read Chapter 9 of the previous book in this series, please consider purchasing a hard copy (available from most major retailers) or the eBook from Amazon. Details are listed on the website:

https://DoctrineParadox.com/order-the-book/

If you cannot afford this book, please send requests to doctrineparadox@gmail.com. I will send you a free copy.

~

For those who have already read the chapter *What Is the Matrix?* [23], you may recall this distinctively unpopular theological statement:

What would you say if I told you, you can know the truth? You can understand very easily the meaning of life on this planet and the purpose for the creation of the universe.

What would you say if I told you, the bible clearly and unobjectionably states the human race existed before the womb/matrix was created?

What would you say if I told you, the reason we are all living in this spiritually deceived existence is the result of mankind's disobedience to our Creator in a former angelic state? [24]

This is certainly not what "the church" teaches. It is much too taboo as it flies in the face of hundreds of years of church tradition. However, it is what the various authors of the Bible had specified on multiple occasions as explained thoroughly in the previous Matrix chapter.

The point of revisiting the Matrix at this stage is to illustrate once again the fact that mankind was created before we entered the Matrix — we were created before we entered our mother's womb.

What is more interesting than using The Matrix as a fictional parallel to describe this world of machinations in which we live, is the fact that the bible does indeed give mention to the "matrix" — by name. Coincidentally, much like *The Matrix* trilogy, the Bible is also referring to a world being pulled over our eyes, similar in part but so very different when given closer scrutiny.

Earlier versions of the Bible including the King James Bible use the word "matrix" or variations in the spelling of the word from the old English dialect such as "matryce" and "matrice." We see this in Exodus chapters 13:12–15; 34:19 and Numbers 3:12; 18:15.

We know how Hollywood portrays *The Matrix*. But how does the Bible explain this mystery? Well, the word "matrix" is only used when referring to the female womb… how very interesting. In the Bible, the portal from which life is brought into this fallen world is introduced to us as "the matrix."

"Matrix"

""7358 {26x} rechem, rekh'-em; from 7355; the womb [comp. 7356]: – womb {21x}, matrix {5x}. Rechem, as a noun, means "bowels; womb; mercy." The first use of rechem is in its primary meaning of womb". [1] "7355 {47x} racham, raw-kham'; a prim. Root; to fondle; by impl. To love, espec. to be compassionate: – mercy {32x}, compassion {8x}, pity {3x}, love {1x}, merciful {1x}, Ruhamah {1x}, surely {1x}. Racham, the verb, means "to have compassion, be merciful, pity" "7356 {44x} racham, rakh'-am; from 7355; compassions (in the plural); by extens. the womb (as cherishing the fetus); by implication a maiden: – mercy {30x}, compassion {4x}, womb {4x}, bowels {2x}, pity {2x}, damsel {1x}, tender love {1x}. Racham expresses a deep and tender feeling of compassion, such as is aroused by the sight of weakness or suffering in those who are deer to us or in need of our help."

This word "matrix," which in the Hebrew tongue is *rechem* (womb), comes from its Hebrew derivative *racham*, which means love, compassion, mercy, to have pity on or cherish a loved one who is weak and suffering. The meaning of the womb (the matrix) most accurately resembles an act of mercy.

Okay…? A person should ask, why is the process of a spirit supernaturally entering the mother's womb, and later, entering into this world explained as an act of compassion, mercy, and pity? What could this possibly mean? [25]

What does it mean to suggest everyone who enters the womb from a prior existence is being shown "mercy, compassion, pity" (racham) in the womb (rechem)? As mentioned in said lengthy chapter, the answer is of course that we all took part in sin, in our former angelic state. This life, the life we are now living in the flesh, is a second chance to repent and seek the Father's will in our lives. The womb (matrix) is referred to as "mercy" because it is in this life that we are offered atonement for our sins and presented with a way back into the Kingdom of God — back into the Garden of Eden. God is showing us compassion by offering *mercy* to those who had betrayed Him, turned away from Him, and sought out to worship other gods.

Several passages of scripture strongly suggest a great multitude of what would ultimately become mankind (metaphorically referred to as a system of "trees") existed in the Garden of Eden alongside "Adam" and "Eve" (Ezekiel 17:12–24; 28:12–13; 31:8–14; Isaiah 14:8–15). These vast nations of "trees" committed a number of heinous sins while in Eden, the Garden of God. Engulfed by their own pride, they would be cast down to earth, to the depths of Sheol (Ezekiel 31:14; Isaiah 14:15; Revelation 12:4).

At some point while still in Eden, Adam and Eve had finally succumbed to the realization of their own transgressions. They chose to hide themselves "among the trees of the garden" (Genesis 3:8).

Our heavenly Father knew these transgressions could not go unpunished. Something needed to be done. Being overcome by His undying love for us, God predestined a plan to die a most gruesome death on our behalf, a sacrificial offering for the sins of His children. The Father would create from His own being, a likeness of Himself. A Christ for all mankind.

"For he shall grow up before him as a tender plant, and as a root out of a dry ground... He is despised and rejected of men; a man of sorrows, and acquainted with grief... Surely he hath borne our griefs and carried our sorrows... but he was wounded for our transgressions, he was bruised for our iniquities: the chastisement of our peace was upon him: and with his stripes we are healed. All we like sheep have gone astray; we have turned every one to his own way; and the Lord hath laid on him the iniquity of us all." (Isaiah 53:2-6; emphasis mine)

Christ, in the image of the Father, entered the matrix (the womb) to be physically born into this world. He grew into a young man who would preach the true gospel message of repentance from sin and the arrival of the kingdom of God (Matthew 3:2; 4:17; Mark 1:15; Luke 10:9). Christ would then fulfill the Father's plan by offering His own blood on the cross and declaring His power over death by rising from the grave. This sacrifice offering paved the way for all who believe in Him to eventually regain access to the eternal "tree" of life (Genesis 2:9; 3:24; Revelation 22:2).

Our purpose in this world is to love God and to love one another as He loves us (John 13:34). To be reconciled back into the Father's kingdom; that is the meaning of life. **[26]**

In addition to this evidence, the reader may recall another statement from the original Matrix chapter many Christian believers will consider outrageous as well.

People often use the name Lucifer synonymously with Satan, or the Devil. But did you know the names Lucifer and Satan are never mentioned in the same passage of scripture? In fact, the name Lucifer (H1966; "title applied to the king of Babylon") is only mentioned one time in the entire bible (Isaiah 14:12) and it is never mentioned as being the same man/angel as Satan. There is no biblical evidence whatsoever to support the notion that Lucifer, is Satan. No such passage exists. The understanding that Lucifer is Satan is implied by modern pop-culture Christianity, television producers, secularism, as well as many unlearned bible teachers. And still, is never once mentioned in the Holy Bible.

The names "Devil" and "Satan" are found in the same passages such as in Revelation 9:12 and 20:2, but never do Lucifer and Satan, nor Lucifer and the Devil, ever show up in the same passage or even in the same context as a reference to the same creature. That is important to note as we look into the book of Isaiah.

The only time the name "Lucifer" ever shows up in the bible, is one time in Isaiah 14 when it is clearly referring to the earthly king of Babylon. **[27]**

Outrageous, but true. The only place you will find evidence to support such a doctrine, that is, Lucifer is Satan, is in the imaginations of the people who conjured up the idea in the first place. That, and Hollywood propaganda of course. We may never know the origins of who first made this claim or why it is so thoroughly entrenched in modern theology, but the fact is this: virtually every Christian theologian on the planet believes this to be the case even though there is no biblical evidence to support the claim.

Notice how in minute mark 5:30 to 6:00 of this video clip [28] MacArthur clearly states, "Lucifer would become Satan." Notice also that he did not provide a single shred of evidence to make this claim. Nobody ever does. They simply state it as a fact that does not need justification or biblical verification. They expect us to take them at their word, without evidence, that Lucifer and Satan are the same creature, that Satan is nothing more than one of God's created angels. But, is this the case?

A person may ask why any of this is important. Who cares if Satan and Lucifer are potentially not the same creature? Biblically, they are both evil, and they are both destined to eternal punishment. Are we splitting hairs for no reason at this point? Absolutely not. It matters a great deal because making this clear and concise distinction between the two entities is at the root of understanding the origins of evil!

How art thou fallen from heaven, O Lucifer, son of the morning! how art thou cut down to the ground, which didst weaken the nations! 13For thou hast said in thine heart, I will ascend into heaven, I will exalt my throne above the stars of God: I will sit also upon the mount of the congregation, in the sides of the north: ¹⁴I will ascend above the heights of the clouds; I will be like the most High. ¹⁵Yet thou shalt be brought down to hell, to the sides of the pit. ¹⁶They that see thee shall narrowly look upon thee, and consider thee, saying, Is this *the man* that made *the earth* to tremble, that did shake kingdoms; ¹⁷That made *the world* as a wilderness, and *destroyed the cities thereof*; that opened not the house of *his prisoners?*" (Isaiah 14:12-17)

In the one single instance where the Bible refers to this entity, Lucifer, it clearly states he is a man, an earthly king who conquered territories, destroyed cities, and enslaved many people. The thing we need to understand is that long before this man was born into a flesh body on earth, he existed as an angel who fell from God's grace while in his former angelic state. Like all other fallen angels, Lucifer was later sent to earth as a punishment for his sins.

...so that all *the trees* by the waters will not be exalted in their stature, nor put their tops among the clouds, nor will any of their well-watered mighty ones stand straight in their height. For they *have all been turned over to death*, to the earth beneath, *among mankind*, with those who go down to the pit. (Ezekiel 31:14; NAS)

So where is all this information leading us? Why place so much emphasis on mankind existing before the whom? Why place so much emphasis on the Bible's definition of "the matrix"? Why place so much emphasis on Satan not being the same entity as Lucifer? Why place so much emphasis on how this fallen angel, Lucifer, like so many others, was later born into the body of a man (Isaiah 14; Ezekiel 28–32)?

In order to further understand the origins of evil, we need to first answer these questions with an understanding that there is more to the Bible than meets the eye. Not least of which, there is much more to the Garden of Eden story than we have been led to believe.

The Parable of the Garden of Eden

Scholars, theologians, musicians, and brutally honest laymen have sought answers for hundreds of years as to whether Eden was a literal habitation on planet earth (i.e., they literally bit into a piece of fruit, made aprons from fig leaves, etc.) or whether the Eden story is divinely constructed as another one of our Lord's parables. Many learned men have argued for and against the clear discrepancies in the creation account (Genesis 1) and the account in the Garden of Eden (Genesis 2, 3).

In the creation account, Adam and Eve were created on the same day (day 6; Genesis 1:27). In the Eden account (Genesis 2, 3), Adam is created first (v.2:7), and then Eve is created much later (v.2:21–22).

In the creation account, man was created after plants and animals at the end of the sixth day (v.1:11–28). In the Eden account (Genesis 2, 3), man was created first — before the plants (v.2:7–9) and before the animals (v.2:18–20).

In the creation account (Genesis 1), there is a vast body of water, the sea (v.1:9). In the Eden account, there is no water other than the mist from the ground and the springs flowing out from Eden, which watered the garden (v.2:5–6).

If we take the account in the Garden of Eden to be literal, and not a parable, then how do we explain the glaring discrepancies between Genesis 1 and Genesis 2 and 3?

Either Genesis 1 or Genesis 2 and 3 were written by two different authors who did not agree with one another, and therefore *were* telling a different account of what took place. Or, Genesis 1 explains the creation of our current heaven and earth, *whereas* Genesis 2 and 3 is a parable about creation and original sin which took place in "the Garden of Eden" before the creation (or recreation) of our current heaven and earth. In other words, both are factual accounts, but they are telling the story of two different events. One is the original creation of the heavens and the earth made to perfection (Genesis 1:1), and the other is the recreated heaven and earth (after the sin events in the Garden of Eden) which was completed in six days (Genesis 1:2–31).

The fact is, there are discrepancies in the creation account if we view the Garden of Eden account to be literally true. However, if we view the Garden of Eden account as a parable, the creation account is flawless.

Most movies and written stories portray a "snake" in the garden because it says "the serpent" was made to "crawl on his belly" for deceiving the woman (Genesis 3:14). Did "the serpent" (Satan) in physical form literally walk up to Eve and talk to her about a "fruit tree" before he was literally turned into a snake? Did Eve open her eyes to the "knowledge of good and evil" the moment she literally bit into "a piece of fruit" such as an apple? Did Adam and Eve literally make loincloths from fig leaves to hide their genitalia? What does the "knowledge of good and evil" and a "piece of fruit" have in common with human genitals in the first place? Ironically, the female genitalia is the doorway to the womb: the matrix, which can only produce life with the seed of a man. Ask yourself, what precisely is the "knowledge of good and evil"? Why does the story then tell us the Lord God put "enmity" between the Devil's seed and Eve's seed (Genesis 3:15)? And, why is the Devil spawning "seed" in the Garden of Eden? Does it have anything to do with Satan creating his own race of humanlike creatures without God's permission (Genesis 6)?

Adam (the first man) had absolutely nothing to do with the transgression until after the woman had partaken of "the fruit" with the Devil. She then brought that "knowledge" to Adam. Could this enmity between the "seeds" be an account of forbidden offspring? Could it be, this whole Garden of Eden account is simply another one of the Lord's many parables?

Dear reader, all throughout the Bible, man and angels are referred to as "trees." Jesus said, we would know the false prophets by "their fruits" (Matthew 7:17–20). He said, "a good tree cannot produce bad fruit." This is one of the many parables taught by the Lord Himself.

Both angels and mankind are referred to as "trees" (Psalm 1:1–3; Jeremiah 17:7–8; Matthew 3:10; 7:15–23; 12:33–37; Mark 4:3–9; Luke 3:9; John 15:4–5; Galatians 5:22; Jude 12; [the Tree of Life: Genesis 2:9, Revelation 22:2]).

The "fig tree" (Adam and Eve covered their genitals with "fig leaves" [Genesis 3:7]) is often used in the Bible to represent Israel, the keepers of the law (Joel 2:21–25; Luke 13:6–9). In this case, we have an entire nation of people referred to as "a fig tree."

"And when he saw a fig tree in the way, he came to it, and found nothing thereon, but leaves only and said unto it, Let no fruit grow on thee henceforward for ever. And presently the fig tree withered away." (Matthew 21:19)

The symbolism here is quite profound. This is at a time when Christ was only days away from fulfilling His mission to sacrifice Himself on the cross. This chastisement of the fig tree took place during His triumphant entrance into Jerusalem. Jesus was hungry and desired something to eat. He then came upon a fig tree on the road into the city. Jesus saw this fig tree was no longer producing fruit. It was only producing leaves. At His spoken Word, the fig tree withered and died right then and there "for ever" (v.19).

What could it possibly mean (if we consider the law in Israel as the "fig tree") to say Jesus made the fig tree in Jerusalem die "for ever"?

Getting back to the Garden of Eden account. Due to "Adam and Eve's" rebellion (eating "fruit" from the "tree" they were not supposed to "eat"), mankind was made to cover themselves (their genitalia) with leaves from a fig tree (the law) until the Father in the personage of Jesus Christ (the tree of Life) came in the flesh to take away the sins of the world. After Jesus did what he did, the law (the fig tree) was no longer required to cover the sins of the people (fig leaves). Jesus had fulfilled the law in his sacrifice. That could be why we see Jesus chastise the fig tree "for ever" in Matthew 21.

It is entirely possible to interpret the parable of Adam and Eve's fig leaf loincloths in this manner. However, a person could spend their whole life unraveling the Eden mystery. It ties into everything, including original sin, salvation, and the nature of our lives on this planet.

Whether we choose to accept the Eden account as a parable or not, one thing is undeniable: The Bible is openly forthcoming when it affirms God speaks to mankind using parables. God then reveals these parables to those who have eyes to see and ears to hear (Isaiah 45:15–19; Matthew 13:1–17).

Whenever mankind and angels are referred to as trees, it is all part of an ongoing parable with roots stretching all throughout the Bible. Why would the account in the Garden of Eden be any different?

The Lord Jesus Christ is the tree of life. Satan is the tree of knowledge of good and evil. The Lord's tree produces good fruit which gives eternal life (Genesis 3:22–24). Satan's tree produces bad fruit which brings death to those who partake of its "fruit" (Genesis 2:17).

There is something about the way in which we teach the Garden of Eden account that just doesn't add up. **[29]**

Notice how, while in the Garden of Eden, Satan was "planting seeds." What this means is that Satan was creating offspring (his children) without God's permission!

The Bible clearly states that God created angels (Psalms 148:1-6; presumably immortal) as well as the "mortals" ("Adam" and "Eve" [humans]), and they were all present in the Garden of Eden. Satan at some point infiltrated God's "garden" (both physically and spiritually speaking) and perverted God's creation by transforming it into something outside the will of God. He turned admiration into jealousy (Genesis 4:1–8). He turned love into hatred (4:5). He turned life into death (v4:8). He turned truth into lies (v4:9). He turned righteousness into evil! (v6:1–4) God did not create evil, Satan did!

Here is the question we desperately need to understand. Why does the atheist cast all the blame for evil on our Loving

Creator God when it was clearly Satan who passed down this evil "knowledge" to Jehovah's creation?

Now then, we know Satan has the power to manipulate Jehovah's creation. This is made clear to us from at least Genesis 3, 6, Job 1–2, and Revelation 12, among other sources. Who is to say Lucifer is not one of Satan's twisted creations? One of the "seeds" Satan had planted in God's "Garden of Eden"? Do you remember this infamous quote?

> Jesus said unto them, *If God were your Father*, ye would love me: for *I proceeded forth and came from God*; neither came I of myself, but he sent me. [43]Why do ye not understand my speech? even because ye cannot hear my word. [44]*Ye are of your father the devil*, and the lusts of your father ye will do. He was a murderer from the beginning, and abode not in the truth, because there is no truth in him. When he speaketh a lie, he speaketh of his own: for *he is a liar, and the father of it*. [45]And because I tell you the truth, ye believe me not. (John 8:42–45)

What is Jesus referring to in this statement? Why did Jesus claim those religious leaders were not children of God? Why did He claim they were in fact children of their father, the Devil? Is that due to the intermingling of "seeds" in the "Garden of Eden"? Is it due to spiritual warfare such as that proposed by Paul in Ephesians 6? Is it due to God hardening their hearts because He cannot stand for their hatred of the truth?

> So I gave them over to the stubbornness of their heart, To walk by their own plans. (Psalms 81:12; NAS)

Why, O Lord, do You cause us to stray from Your ways And harden our heart from fearing You? Return for the sake of Your servants, the tribes of Your heritage. (Isaiah 63:17)

He hath blinded their eyes, and hardened their heart; that they should not see with their eyes, nor understand with their heart, and be converted, and I should heal them. [41]These things said Esaias, when he saw his glory, and spake of him. (John 12:40–41)

And for this cause God shall send them strong delusion, that they should believe a lie. (2 Thessalonians 2:11)

O Timothy, keep that which is committed to thy trust, avoiding profane and vain babblings, and oppositions of science falsely so called. (1 Timothy 6:20)

Could it be simply that God has hardened the heart of the unbeliever due to their reluctance to hear the potential for truth? They cling to their "theories" searching for answers in their philosophies and the "nothingness" of a pre-creation as well as the "why" of evil, all the while ignoring the physical scientific evidence which proves creation was endowed by a mighty and loving creator **[18] [19] [20] [21] [22]**.

~

The Sum of the Whole

First, the account in the Garden of Eden is one of the Lord's many parables. It should not be interpreted as literal imagery. If literal, it would be contradicting Genesis 1, and therefore, we would need to explain such glaring discrepancies between the two accounts.

Second, "mankind"; both fallen angels and sinful men and women (mortals) took part in rebelling against the will of God, leading to sin. This all happened while living in the Garden of Eden. Moreover, it all happened before the current universal construction ever took place. God then recreated everything in six days, just as it says in Genesis 1. It is made clear throughout the Bible that God knew us "before we were born" (Isaiah 51:1; Peter 1:2; Ephesians 1:4–11; Romans 8:29; 2 Timothy 1:9; Revelation 13:8).

> All who live on the earth will worship him, everyone whose name has not been written since the foundation of the world in the book of life of the Lamb who has been slaughtered. (Revelation 13:8; NAS)

Why are the names of the redeemed in Christ written in the book of life before the foundations of the world? Why were the rest of the names excluded? Why was the "Lamb" destined to be slaughtered before the world began?

> Before I formed you in the womb I knew you; Before you were born I sanctified you; I ordained you a prophet to the nations. (Jeremiah 1:5; NKJ)

According as he hath chosen us in him before the foundation of the world, that we should be holy and without blame before him in love: ⁵Having predestinated us unto the adoption of children by Jesus Christ to himself, according to the good pleasure of his will. (Ephesians 1:4–5)

As much as Christians refuse to believe it, or are unable to see the forest through the trees, we all existed before we entered into this flesh. The Bible claims we existed before the womb. We existed before we entered "the matrix."

Third, Satan and Lucifer are not the same creature. No one can or has ever offered proof to suggest Lucifer is the same creature as Satan. Why? Because there is no evidence to prosecute the defendant. There is no proof to present to the judge or jury. It should all be thrown out as a mistrial.

In closing, we need to understand that once again, the burden of proof comes into play, one way or the other; both sides need to prove or disprove the claims they are espousing. How have we created such a dogmatic unbreakable theology regarding something so biblically unsubstantiated?

Similar to atheism, Christianity has in many cases crossed a line into doctrinal "theory." So, if we are now permitted to simply create new theories and institute them as official church doctrine, who is to stop someone from bucking the status quo of modern theology by asking new questions?

For instance, where is the biblical evidence to claim Satan is one of God's creations?

CHAPTER 4

Satan's Realm–God's Realm

Please allow this chapter to saturate your skepticism for a brief moment. After the evidence is brought forward, you are welcome to retreat to your former way of thinking. The reader has nothing to fear other than a friendly debate one way or the other. You can always label this author a heretic, blasphemer, even a damned idiot who refuses to adopt scientific theory. Let us play the "devil's advocate," as they say, by entertaining the following statement:

~

There is no biblical evidence to suggest Jehovah created Satan.

~

Those who commonly read the Bible should immediately reject such a notion and recall this familiar passage of scripture:

> Now the serpent was more subtil than any beast of the field which the LORD God had made. (Genesis 3:1)

Think about this sentence logically. Does it say Satan literally *is* one of the "beasts of the field"? No, it says Satan is "more subtil" than the beasts of the field. Does it say God created "the serpent"? No, it says God created the "beasts of the field." It calls Satan a "serpent" (H5175; *nāḥāš*; nahash; to hiss) which is not the same Hebrew word as "beast" (H2416; *ḥay*; chay; "alive" or "living creature"). The "beasts" (chay) are a living, breathing "alive" creature that God created during His initial phase of creation. This other entity, the "serpent" (nahash), is something entirely different. Scrutiny of this passage will reveal greater insight to this mystery. These two creatures are clearly not the same "kind" or "type" of creature.

Serpent
"נָחָשׁ m.-(1) *a serpent*, so called from its hissing (see the root) Gen. 3:1, seq.; Ex. 4:3; 7:15; 2 Ki. 18:4. Used of the constellation of the serpent or dragon in the northern part of the sky, Arab. (2) [Nahash, pr. n.—(a) of a town otherwise unknown, 1 Ch. 4:12.-(b) of a king of the Ammonites, 1 Sam. 11.1; 2 Sam. 10:2, and of various men.-(c) 2 Sa. 17:27.-(d) 2 Sa. 17:25." **[30]**

Beast

"חַי {501x} chay, *khah'-ee*; from 2421; *alive*; hence, raw (flesh); fresh (plant, water, year), stong; also (as noun, espec. In the fem. Sing. And masc. plur.) life (or living thing), whether lit. or fig.:-live" **[31]**

Let us not forget how this entire "Garden of Eden" episode is a parable. This passage of scripture *never* claims God created the serpent. We who read the Bible are only *implying* that God created the serpent. The only potential proof to suggest God created Satan is Genesis 1-2 or John 1 where it stated God created everything in heaven (the physical universe) and earth. But who is to say Satan originated in the Lord God's creation—in His "heaven and earth"? Who is to say Satan originated in the same dimension or realm as the physical "Garden of Eden" that God created to perfection? If Jehovah's creation was a perfect "paradise," why was there a blemish (Satan)? If there is evidence to suggest Satan was created by Jehovah, please present the evidence. This is not a trick question. It is a charge brought against the believer and a challenge brought forward to the reader. Where is the proof? Where in the Bible does it say God created Satan?

Furthermore, where in the Bible does it say our Loving Creator God is the only Creator who exists in the eternal realms? Eternal realms, by the way, which we know absolutely nothing about. Be honest with yourself. Are we not only *assuming* that God created "the dragon, *old serpent, which is the Devil, and Satan*"? (Revelation 20:2)

Let us take the *why* out of the equation. Please provide biblical evidence to suggest *how* and *when* God Himself created "the dragon" and all his evil ways.

Furthermore, there is no biblical evidence to suggest God (H3068; *Yᵊhōvâ*) is the only entity to exist in the eternal "realms." Notice the plurality of the statement. Realm(s), with an (s), plural. Multiple realms.

> ...he exerted when he raised Christ from the dead and seated him at his right hand in the *heavenly realms*" (Ephesians 1:20; NIV)

Notice also the distinction between the "heavenly realms" where God summoned His own resurrected son Jesus and that of Satan's inhabitance within the same "heavenly realms."

> For our struggle is not against flesh and blood, but against the rulers, against the authorities, against the powers of this dark world and against the spiritual forces of *evil in the heavenly realms.* (Ephesians 6:12; NIV)

> I know a man in Christ who fourteen years ago was caught up to *the third heaven.* (2 Corinthians 12:2; NIV)

Ephesians 6:12 clearly states there is "*evil* in the heavenly realms." This is contrary to what we Christians have learned about heaven. They tell us heaven is a never-ending blissful harmony of peace and serenity. Once again, are we not only assuming God is the one and only entity to exist in eternity and that the "third heaven" is the last rung of the ladder? Who is to say there is not a fourth, fifth, or one-millionth heaven?

~

We portray our creator God as a singular eternal entity who apparently got lonely and then at some point decided He wanted to create two companions — Adam and Eve. Once Tweedledum and Tweedledee were presented with a satanic lie; oops! God messed up! He made a mistake by creating free will, and as a result, much to His dismay, evil is now ever-present in His creation. And if that is the case, wouldn't that mean our Loving Creator God is not without the capacity to make a mistake? (Genesis 6:6)

Who is to say our existence is the one and only existence spawned from eternity? To suggest so is a rather vain philosophy, don't you think? Is eternity so small that we humans are the only existence?

As an example, consider scientific theory which suggests we came from nothing and nowhere and were created by no one. Who is to say there are not an infinite amount of "nothings" that inevitably spawned creations of their own. This is the exact theory behind the multiverse proposition.

Back down here on planet earth, we have a parallel universe known to us as the realm of imagination, aka scientific theory, wherein, many devout believers have latched on to the "multiverse" theory that proposes an estimated ten dimensions. The first three dimensions are known as space: the X, Y, and Z axes. The fourth dimension is thought to be time. With these first four dimensions, we can calculate and measure space and time scientifically. The superstring theory comes into play with the fifth dimension. This would introduce the possibility of a mirror image world of similar proportions to our own, yet slightly different. In the sixth dimension, multiple universes are proposed. Here, they introduce the possibility of multiple worlds similar to our own that all have the same origins but did not take the same course of action at any specific point in time. With this, there could be a countless amount of possibilities and a virtually infinite amount of parallel universes. If you remember the TV show *Sliders* from the 1990s, you'll have a good example of what the proposed multiverse theory would look like. The seventh dimension is similar to the sixth dimension barring the fact that these multiple universes would not have the same origins. They would all have had different origins (once again taking God out of the equation), which would in turn create an even larger capacity for infinite possibilities. The eighth, ninth, and tenth dimensions are so silly we will not bother covering them except to say they are proposing infinite infinities.

If this sounds a lot like science fiction, that's because it is. Yet, this *is* what passes for "science" these days (1 Timothy 6:20). This author is obviously not suggesting the multiverse theory with its estimated ten dimensions is correct. He only wishes to illustrate what a real "multiple dimensions" would look like with an existing creator God, as opposed to God *not* existing, that is, the multiverse theory, the big bang theory, the fake science of evolution, the religion of atheism, and so on.

Now, in the realm of proposed theoretical "church doctrine," to which the remaining chapters are dedicated, it should be noted once again how the burden of proof resides on both sides of the argument. This author will state his argument as succinctly as possible where the skeptical Christian (and atheist) will need to refute, and vice versa. Due to there being little-to-no evidence to disprove the ideas written herein, we need to acknowledge the fact that the burden of proof exists for everyone. For instance, the doctrine of Lucifer and Satan being the same creature is unproven and unbiblical; and yet, it exists nonetheless.

Is it heresy to bring this fact out into the light of day?

Is it heresy to suggest there might be other existences outside our own?

Is there any biblical evidence to suggest there are *not* multiple dimensions or multiple realms in eternity?

Is there any biblical evidence to suggest there are not other "gods" who wish to infringe upon Jehovah's creation, in *His* dimension? If so, bring the evidence forward. Prove it.

As mentioned, the burden of proof is a double-edged sword. It is a coin with two sides.

If it is true to suggest God is the only God in the enteral realms (outside of our physical universe), why did He command the Israelites, "Thou shalt have no other gods before me" (Exodus 20:3)?

If our God is the only God, why did He tell us not to worship other gods? It makes a person wonder. Who are these other "gods," and where did they come from?

We know the Hebrew word for "gods" used in this passage is (H430; *elohiym*) which can indicate any number of *gods* in the ordinary sense: but spec. used (in the plur. Thus, espec. With the art.) of the supreme *God*; occasionally applied by ways of deference to *magistrates*; and sometimes as a superlative: God" [32]

Who is to say Satan is not also one of these "gods" (elohiym) who are known to exist from eternity and, in this case, exist in other realms or dimensions? Or else, does it not state in Genesis 3:22, "And the LORD God said, Behold, the man is become as **one of us**, to know good and evil"? Who exactly is the "us" in this passage (and in Genesis 1:26), and who exactly is God talking to? Is God talking to Himself? Is God talking to the "trinity"? Is God talking to Satan? Or is God talking to one (or many) of the other "gods" who exist in His original eternal plane of existence — the dimensions of "eternity"? Exactly how many gods are there other than *our* creator God, Jehovah? That, we do not know.

What we do know is that it was Satan's actions that caused the angels to fall from grace (Revelation 12). After Satan did what he did, these fallen angels began lifting themselves to the status of being equal or even *better* than Jehovah (Isaiah 14). We know Satan shares this sentiment of being better than Jehovah, but the Bible never says Satan is one of the angels Jehovah created! That is the point. Satan is not one of God's creations!

Again, the thinking that God created Satan is implied by us, the reader. The Bible only ever refers to Satan as "the dragon, that old serpent, which is the Devil, and Satan" (Revelation 20:1) and yet never refers to Satan as anything other than himself — the creator of deception and evil.

What we also know about Satan is that we have no idea where Satan came from. We do not know Satan's origin. The Bible never clarifies this point except to say he is an "old serpent."

Who is to say "nothing" exists outside our current universal creation when the Bible clearly says otherwise? The Bible says eternity, and "heavenly realms" *do* exist outside our physical realm (Genesis 1–3; Ephesians 1:20; 6:12; 2 Corinthians 12:2; Revelation). Who is to say this one existence (our current physical universe) is the only physical universe to ever burst forth from eternity? If there is evidence to suggest this is the case, please bring that evidence forward to silence this burdened soul.

Is God the only eternal entity with the ability to create? If so, prove it.

~

We should also introduce the concept of trespassing. Trespassing is to enter a territory without permission. A posted sign reads "Private Property. No Trespassing! Violators will be Prosecuted!" But that will never stop a criminal from entering the territory and doing as they please, will it? The criminal will do whatsoever they please with no

regard for law and order. Who is to say there are no criminals in "eternal realms" or "heavenly realms"?

When a person is caught breaching the boarders of private
property, they are thrown into jail for breaking the laws of
that territory. Who is to say trespassing does not also exist in
eternity? Who is to say "the dragon, that old serpent, which
is the Devil, and Satan" did not exist in some other realm
before he trespassed into Jehovah's "realm" or "dimension"
or "creation," whatever you want to call it. After trespassing,
Satan was caught doing what he knew he was not permitted
to do, and now he is being eternally judged by the creator
of *this* realm. Satan is currently in the trial phase of his sen-
tencing (this current universal construction). Soon, his final
sentence will be carried out (the new heaven and earth).

> And he laid hold on the dragon, that old serpent, which is
> the Devil, and Satan, and bound him a thousand years…
> And *the devil that deceived them* was cast into the lake of fire
> and brimstone, where the beast and the false prophet are,
> and shall be tormented day and night for ever and ever.
> (Revelation 20:2; 10)

~

A student of the Bible will also remember this familiar
passage of scripture:

> And the LORD God commanded the man, saying, Of
> every tree of the garden thou mayest freely eat: [17]But of
> the tree of the knowledge of good and evil, thou shalt not

eat of it: for in the day that thou eatest thereof thou shalt surely die. (Genesis 2:16–17)

Clearly, God was familiar with this evil "tree" existing in His garden, which would mean He was aware of evil even before He began creating, right? He was aware of it even before "the fall from grace," right? And since this "tree" was in God's garden, God must have created it, right? Well, no. That is another very misleading false assumption.

Ask yourself, why would God openly call out these two "trees" specifically by name, and yet not one single tree other than these two trees are ever called out or given a specific name? What could the significance of these two "trees" possibly represent?

> Now the Lord God had planted a garden in the east, in Eden; and there he put the man he had formed. [9]The Lord *God made all kinds of trees* grow out of the ground — *trees that were pleasing* to the eye *and good for food*. In the middle of the garden were the tree of life and *the tree of* the knowledge of good and *evil*. (Genesis 2:8–9)

If we take this statement at face value, it is an unsolvable paradox. It would be a direct contradiction in itself. In this passage, it clearly says God made all the trees that were "pleasing" and "good for food." It then explains that there was also a tree "in the middle of the garden" that was "evil." Let us don our logical thinking caps. How could God state all the trees He made were "pleasing" and "good for food" while at the same time stating one of the trees He created was good "and evil"? Furthermore, if every single tree God had made was "good for food," why did He command Adam to never "eat" from this one specific "tree"? The answer is so obvious it is downright embarrassing to learn theologians have yet to make the connection. The answer to this paradoxical contradiction is that it is not a paradox at all. God did *not* create the tree of "knowledge of good and evil." That "tree" originated somewhere else!

The "tree of life" (God Himself in the personage of Jesus Christ; Revelation 22:14; John 6) and the "tree of knowledge of good and evil" (Satan and his knowledge of deception) both existed from eternity. This would have been a time before Jehovah ever began His current creation—us. The reason these two "trees" are the only two trees called out by name is because they existed *before* the creation of all the *other* trees in the garden. The trees that were "pleasing" and "good for food" were created *during* the Eden account.

Remember, this is a parable of "trees" with roots stretching all throughout the Bible. The parable of mankind and angels being "trees" is in multiple books written by multiple authors over multiple centuries. This is explained in detail in the original Matrix chapter.

Notice this one very interesting detail concerning the parable:

The Lord Jesus Christ is the tree of life. Satan is the tree of knowledge of good and evil. The Lord's tree produces good fruit which gives eternal life (Genesis 3:22–24). Satan's tree produces bad fruit which brings death to those who partake of its "fruit." (Genesis 2:17) **[33]**

Since this is the case, we know the "trees" Jehovah intentionally called out by name are (1) the selfsame eternal, self-existent word of God, His begotten son, Jesus Christ, and (2) the deceptive eternal entity known to us as "Satan" the "old serpent."

A person could suggest Genesis 2:16–17 is evidence that God did in fact create Satan because it can most certainly be proven that Jehovah is the only entity with original powers of creation existing in "the Garden of Eden." However, it would appear Satan does have the ability to manipulate God's creation. The idea of Satan being created *in* the Garden of Eden is only speculation, if not entirely imagination. Once we acknowledge this "tree" is not a tree at all but is in fact a very deceptive eternal creature who is only *referred to* as a "tree" in this parable, the paradigm changes. If this tree is an eternal creature, that means he was not created by God. Whenever and wherever he was created, it was not in "the Garden of Eden." It would have been somewhere else, in a different "realm" or "dimension." This would also mean Satan existed before this creation (Jehovah's creation) ever took place.

Satan *is* like God in the sense that God existed before our physical creation. "Our," being a creation that only took place in "the Garden of Eden." Satan is a "tree" who broke the rules by trespassing into the Garden with the intention of meddling with Jehovah's creation. Meddling: mayhem, mischief, murder, and mystery. All in a day's work for the creator of evil.

This is the second of "four solutions" mentioned in the introduction.

God did not create Satan. Satan is *not* one of the "mortals." Satan is an eternal being like Jehovah but does not share Jehovah's morals or values. Satan is a deceptive, treacherous criminal whose desire is to infiltrate and destroy what does not and never did belong to him. In this case, Satan seeks to destroy Jehovah's love for His creation.

Just like a criminal arsonist in our physical realm would break into a building only to burn it to the ground for no other reason than "because I felt like it," he just wanted to, so he did. Satan broke into God's territory and perverted Jehovah's creation, and now he is stuck here. At some point Jehovah said, *no way, I cannot allow this.* Hell was then created as a result of Satan's trespassing and intermingling of the "seeds" in God's Garden of Eden.

> Then He will say to those on His left, "Depart from Me, you who are cursed, into the eternal fire *prepared for the devil and his angels.*" (Matthew 25:41; NIV)

Notice, not in this passage nor any other passage of the Bible does it ever state the Devil *is* an angel. It does say however that the Devil *has* angels who follow him. If not all, then a great majority of these angels were created by God (and perhaps some were created by Satan [Genesis 3:15]). They existed in the "Garden of Eden" (Ezekiel 28–32). Later, they fell from grace by following the Devil's deceptive ways (Revelation 12; Jude; 2 Peter 2:4). Satan is now doomed to the earth, and he will soon be cast into prison for breaking the rules of Jehovah's realm (Revelation 20:1–2).

~

We could go on and on and on like this for several pages explaining all the fine-tuned details of this proposed doctrinal theory; but I will resist. This author assumes he may be required to rebut many attacks in further publications. That is acceptable. Such a bridge will be crossed when it is inevitable. The point here is to make the following distinction as clear as possible. The burden of proof is a paradox. How can a person disprove what this author has written in these pages? How can this author prove what he himself has claimed other than the evidence written herein? That is, there is no biblical evidence to suggest God created Satan, but there is biblical evidence to suggest Satan created evil. Therefore, drumroll please… if our *Loving Creator God* did *not* create Satan, He therefore also did not create evil! God is not to blame for evil. Satan is!

The skeptic will argue, "If God has foreknowledge, and God created Satan, that would mean God knew He was creating evil." Hence, the paradox of "why." *Why* did God knowingly foresee and create Satan's treasonous ways?

They ask *why*… but what if God did not create Satan? What if foreknowledge is not what we think it is? What if free will is not what we think it is? What if Satan's existence comes from a completely separate eternal realm?

To propose the question *"why* does evil exist" is misleading. A person would be making assumptions and asking the wrong questions based on those false assumptions.

How does evil exist? This is the correct question to ask.

Evil exists because Satan is an eternal criminal that trespassed into Jehovah's territory only to subvert our creator's will while turning the hearts of God's loving creatures away from their creator.

This *is* the answer to the ultimate question. Jehovah did not create Satan in the same way angels and mankind were created because he, Satan, came from "eternity." Whatever eternity represents, and wherever eternity exists, that is where Jehovah and Satan were created. Who is to say they are the only two beings in eternity?

Eternity does not have a beginning. It just is and always was. It simply exists. Satan existed before Jehovah's creation (us). Satan entered into Jehovah's realm from somewhere else in the eternal "heavenly realms." He illegally broke into the Garden of Eden and began meddling with Jehovah's creation. This outside force meddling with Jehovah's creation is the origin of evil. Hence, our Loving Creator God did not created evil. Satan did.

Before we close this section, we should address one more passage in the book of Isaiah that could appear to some as a major flaw in this theory—Isaiah 45:7. In the King James Version, it states God "creates evil." In other publications, it states God "allows disaster." In others still the passage states, "I make peace and create calamity" (NKJV). What are we to make of this passage? A person could point to the English version of the King James Bible and say, "Ah Ha! God created evil! It says so in Isaiah 45:7!" But does it? Was the Bible written in English? Is that what the original text indicates?

This word "evil" is the Hebrew word "ra" (H7451; עַר *raʻ*, *rah*) which can mean "bad, evil, adversity, affliction, calamity, displeased, distress, exceeding grief," and so on. We already know God does in fact "create calamity" or "distress" after reading, for instance, the plagues in Egypt. God Himself summoned the plagues ("ra," "evil," "calamity," "distress") upon Pharaoh and his multitudes due to Pharaoh's unwillingness to repent and allow God's people to be set free.

God did not create evil (ra) in the sense that God is the origin of evil in His own creation. Satan is that origin. God summoned "ra" (evil) upon Satan's *re*creation only as a result of the fall from grace (caused by Satan). And He will do all His goodwill and pleasure (even allow "ra" to occur) to ensure His plan (salvation through Christ) comes to pass.

In conclusion, everything stated above is the very "burden of proof" that evil is not a result of a "malevolent bully God" but in fact a result of Satan meddling in Jehovah's *perfect loving harmony*. If you believe you have evidence to suggest an alternative to the evidence presented in this book, I would encourage you to start a conversation by leaving a comment on the blog.

https://doctrineparadox.com/2023/03/21/the-evil-god-of-love/

~

We should also discuss "hellfire" before we go any further.

The common perception is that when God sends a person to hell, they will be tortured for all eternity with pain and suffering never to be extinguished. Going back to the George Carlin effect mentioned in the previous book **[34]**, why would a supposedly loving creator do such a thing? Well, the short answer is, He wouldn't. Hell's fire was never a part of God's original plan, that is, until after Satan broke the mold by perverting Jehovah's creation. Hell was never "on God's mind" until after Satan's deceitful trespassing and lawlessness. Once Satan did what he did, it was necessary to build a prison for those who chose to follow Satan's criminal acts. This prison is known to us mortals as geenna (G1067; *geenna*; outer darkens; hell's fire).

Even so, why would a God of love issue such a harsh punishment? Forever is a very long time when there is nothing but pain and suffering to deal with. Why is there a need to punish so severely the mortals that He Himself foresaw and created?

To answer this question, we need to understand the mortality of eternal beings is nonexistent—they cannot "die" in the sense that we mortals understand. The mortality of created beings however does exist. The mortals of mankind can and do die as a result of sin in the Garden of Eden. However, the Bible never claims hell was created for the mortals. That too would be an assumed man-made teaching. Geenna, or eternal punishment, was created for Satan and his angels (Matthew 25:41). Furthermore, hell was only created *after*

Satan began meddling in God's perfect harmony. Geenna was never a part of Jehovah's original plan! It only became a part of the plan after Satan's nefarious meddling.

But what about this concept of burning forever in eternal agony? Consider how Jesus and John the Baptist both mentioned how a "tree" that does not produce good fruit will be cut down and thrown into the fire (Matthew 3:10; 7:19). That much is pretty clear. But what exactly happens to a tree when it is thrown into a fire? Does the tree burn for all eternity? No, it burns for a while until there is nothing left to burn. It ceases to exist. It does not burn forever and ever; that is impossible. However, the Devil and his angels are sent to eternal punishment because they are eternal beings (presumably immortal) and therefore cannot die. Those among "mankind" in the Garden of Eden are the "mortals" spoken of in the Bible. They are the beings who will partake in the "second death." Satan and his followers are the "immortals" or "his children" who are so unthinkably treacherous that they do in fact deserve this punishment. Immortals go to "eternal punishment," while mankind ceases to exist. The reason they cease to exist is that the body is "burned up" like a "tree" after being thrown into the eternal fire. It is the fire that burns forever, not that which is thrown into the fire.

A created being is not eternal. If it were, it would not have had a beginning date or "creation" date. For instance, the physical universe is *not* eternal. The physical universe itself is mortal. One day, everything we see when we look up into the night sky will cease to exist (Isaiah 65:17; 2 Peter 3:13; Revelation 21:1).

God created the universe. In the same way, God created people. A created being cannot "burn for all eternity" any more than the universe itself can "burn for all eternity."

> Looking for and hasting unto the coming of the day of God, wherein the heavens being on fire shall be dissolved, and the elements shall melt with fervent heat. (2 Peter 3:12)

Even though some passages in the Bible will suggest an "eternal torture" known as "hell," where people will "burn for all eternity," for example, 2 Thessalonians 1:9, there is in fact substantial evidence to the contrary. Mortal beings (created non-eternal beings) are not going to "burn for all eternity in hell's fire" but will in fact cease to exist once thrown into "hell." There is also no evidence to prove such a scenario will be quick and painless. On the contrary, there is evidence to suggest it will likely be more excruciating than the subject could have ever imagined.

> And do not fear those who kill the body but cannot kill the soul. Rather fear him who can *destroy both soul and body in hell*. (Matthew 10:28; NKJ)

What does it mean to suggest both the soul and body can be "destroyed" in hell?

destroy
"ἀπόλλυμι {92x} **apóllymi**, *ap-ol'-loo-mee*; from 575 and the base of 3639; to *destroy* fully (refl. to *perish*, or *lose*), lit. or fig.:"

"*Appolumi* signifies (1) '"to destroy utterly"'" **[35]**

When we cremate a deceased family member (a mortal human body) by committing it to the flame, it does not burn for all eternity. It burns for a few minutes and then ceases to exist. Notice how Jesus states the body *and* soul will both be "destroyed." Remember how "Adam" only became a living "soul" when God "breathed breath into his nostrils."

> And the LORD God formed man of the dust of the ground, and breathed into his nostrils *the breath of life*; and man became a living soul. (Genesis 2:7)

Who is to say God cannot remove this "breath" from our nostrils? This word *breath* (H5397: nᵊšāmâ) literally means a "breathing being."

If God were to remove His breath/spirit, it would render the "soul/body" nonexistent once they enter the fire. It would no longer be a "breathing being." Once our creator God eternally disavows us due to following Satan, the "spirit" we once possessed (either from Satan's seed or from God's seed) will no longer be ours to possess. We will cease to exist. Our spirit itself is a mortal creation.

> At the back of this objection lies a mental picture of heaven and hell co-existing in unilinear time as the histories of England and America co-exist: so that at each moment the blessed could say 'The miseries of hell are *now* going on.' But I notice that Our Lord, while stressing the terror of hell with unsparing severity, usually emphasizes the idea not of a duration but of *finality*." **[36]**

What this means is that there is a "second death" for everyone who does not inherit eternal life. This "second death" is mentioned in several biblical passages — Revelation 2:11; 20:6; 20:14; 21:8; and James 5:20, to name a few.

In John chapter 6, it states a person can "live forever" if they eat the "bread" that Jesus will give them. But what happens if Jesus never gives a person this "bread of life"? Jesus makes a similar claim about water when speaking to the Samaritan woman at Jacob's well (John 4:10), as well as in His promise of eternal life in Revelation 21:6.

Eternal life is brought up by several biblical authors, naturally, by God Himself. If there is in fact eternal life, wouldn't that mean there is also eternal death? What happens to a "soul" or "spirit" after it dies? Same thing that happens to the body. It burns up and ceases to exist. The spirit that was "breathed into our nostrils" belongs to God. Who is to say we are permitted to keep the spirit of God after this "second death"? It seems rather contrary to suggest God's given spirit will burn in hell, don't you think?

> He who has an ear, let him hear what the Spirit says to the churches. He who overcomes shall not be hurt by the second death. (Revelation 2:11; NKJ)

> Blessed and holy is he that hath part in the first resurrection: on such the second death hath no power. (Revelation 20:6)

Wouldn't it be reasonable to suggest this "second death" is the death of the assumed "immortal" spirit? Hence, the spirit/soul/body does not burn for all eternity. It simply ceases to exist once it is thrown into God's eternal flame. And therefore, we can know God is *not* as cruel as the atheists' propaganda proposes. God did not predestine a plan for the eternal punishment of souls who refuse to submit to His authority, as George Carlin used to say. In fact, it is the opposite. Jehovah offers redemption for all souls who broke His rules and followed Satan's rebellion. God allows us to become a part of His family, to reject Satan once and for all and *return* again into His Kingdom!

~

So, *how* does evil exist? It exists as a result of Satan infiltrating Jehovah's domain, His realm, His creation, for the sole purpose of doing what Satan does best: lie, deceive, and destroy. Hence, God did not create evil as the atheists claim. It is that outsider, that intruder, that infiltrator, that trespasser, that original rebel, Satan, that so-named "old serpent," who introduced the concept of evil into God's realm. The only thing the Lord our God should be blamed for is creating perfect love in perfect harmony, a harmony which has *the capacity to be hurt* by evil if and when evil is introduced by an outside force. The presentation of all the worlds' pain and suffering, and inevitable death, is a result of "the dragon, that old serpent, which is the Devil, and Satan" lying, deceiving, and perverting Jehovah's creation. Satan is the origin of all evil in existence. He existed outside God's creative capacity, on his own eternal accord. He trespassed into a realm where

Jehovah was creating and began his work of deception and *re*creation. Due to his eternal crimes, he has now been sentenced to eternal damnation (G1067; *geenna*; outer darkens; hell's fire).

Ironically, while the atheists point their finger at our Loving Creator God to wonder why there is so much evil in the world, they continue to worship the father of lies by believing in and practicing his satanic religion of atheism, fake science, the big bang, evolution, and *self*-willed governance.

Praise be to Lord our God, the creator of Heaven and earth. Praise be to our Lord Jesus Christ. To Him be the glory forever, and forever. Amen.

CHAPTER 5

The Origin of Foreknowledge

The question of "why" once again presents itself when addressing the potential of God's foreknowledge and sovereignty. It is now worth asking once again, why are we asking *why*. "Why" creates the presupposition that we are in fact addressing a fact. "Why" creates the assumption that we are asking on behalf of a known truth with absolute assurance when we could very well be addressing nothing more than a multitude of false assumptions. One such assumption is this: we assume the Lord our God knew Satan was going to do what he did before it happened. We assume Jehovah knew every one of Satan's trickeries before He began creating mankind in the Garden of Eden. And therefore, God allowed it to happen knowing full well that He would need to punish His future creation with "hell's fire" as a result of Satan's rebellion.

Did you know Satan is a liar? Did you know he is also "the father of lies"? (John 8:44) Who is to say Satan would communicate the truth to his eternal companion, Jehovah, in *any* case? Who are we to claim God can read Satan's mind? Who are we to claim Satan would have been telling Jehovah the truth about his intentions in God's garden?

Be honest, are we not only *assuming* God knew Satan's plans in advance? If this is not an assumption, and Jehovah did in fact know Satan's plans even before He began creating, please provide biblical evidence to support that theory; please leave a comment **[37]**. Did God have foreknowledge of how Satan would be "planting seeds" in His garden? If so, show us the evidence. Show us the scriptures to prove it.

What does it mean to suggest the Lord repented and felt grief for creating mankind?

> And it repented the LORD that he had made man on the earth, and it grieved him at his heart. (Genesis 6:6)

This word "repented" (H5162; *nāḥam*) simply means "to be sorry" and "to make a change in one's behaviors."

If God were in possession of foreknowledge *before* creation began, why did He continue creating knowing that He would be subjecting Himself to pain, heartache, and the need for repentance? Is God a masochist who loves torturing Himself? (Isaiah 53:8–10; Matthew 27:27–31)

Why would the LORD foreknowingly create the need for repentance? Aren't we only assuming that God foresaw the existence of evil infiltrating His realm of creation?

We know for certain foreknowledge exists at this current point in time—here in *this* physical realm. In the physical universe that we occupy, God can see all things at once because He exists outside the axis of space and time. So yes, we know God has foreknowledge in *this* creation. But who is to say God also has foreknowledge in the eternal realms?

Couldn't it be possible to suggest God only has foreknowledge in His own personal creation? Furthermore, who is to say the creator God who created us is also the sole source of creation in the eternal realms? Where is the biblical evidence to suggest God is all alone in eternity? Where in the Bible does it say God created eternity itself?

This is the third of "four solutions" mentioned in the introduction.

Before God created anything at all, His intentions were absolutely pure, loving, and virtuous. He did not begin creation knowing ahead of time that Satan would do what he did. Therefore, God is not the "malevolent bully" that Dawkins so methodically stresses in his books.

Our creator God is Himself a victim of Satan's treacheries, which could very well be why God "repented" His creation (Genesis 6:6).

God did not intend for evil to exist. He did not have foreknowledge of Satan's plans. Satan is a very deceptive creature residing from eternity. Similar to Jehovah, Satan existed in eternal realms *before* the creation of mankind.

God is to eternal love what Satan is to eternal deception and hatred.

God did not know Satan would begin "planting seeds" in His Garden of Eden, in turn causing perversion.

Jehovah's Spirit is the spirit of pure love. Ironically, that could very well be the exact reason why evil exists. Jehovah' capacity to love is so pure that even He could not comprehended the existence of what Satan would eventually do and what had begun welling up in His creation, that is, until after the point when Satan began his meddling.

Hence, God said, *Okay, Adam. You see that "tree" over there? That is not one of my "trees," and it is very, very bad for you. That "tree" is very dangerous. I command you, do not "eat" from that "tree"! If you do, very, very bad things will happen. If you "eat" the "fruit" from that "tree," you are literally going to die. Don't do that!* (Genesis 2:16)

Jehovah did not have foreknowledge during His original creation in the Garden of Eden (Genesis 1:1). After Satan convinced one-third of God's created beings to rebel against their creator (by this point in time [Genesis 3:24; Revelation 12], evil had now occurred without God's permission, foreknowledge, or oversight), God devised a universal plan to save that which was lost (Luke 19:10).

It was only after that "time" that God *re*created the universe in six days (Genesis 1:2–31). From this point forward, God had foreknowledge (predestination) because He knew how every single one of His created beings had acted upon Satan's treachery. Some of them followed Satan, while the majority stayed loyal to Jehovah. Before this recreation event, all sin in the Garden of Eden had already taken place. The damage was done. This is *how* predestination and foreknowledge are made possible.

How does Jehovah know things before they happen in our physical realm? Because these events have already happened!

One who seeks the truth must at some point attempt to understand Eternity. We do not see time as our Creator sees time. He exists in a realm where space and time are non-existent. He knows all things throughout time, all at once. That is the very essence of eternity. He knew He was going to come to earth and die as a righteous sacrifice even before He created the current heaven and earth. And He knew exactly what needed to be done to fulfill His sacrifice for our sins. He knew each one of us who would repent, and each one of us who would not. He knew the believers even before the foundations of the earth were laid (Galatians 1:15; Ephesians 1:4–11; 1 Peter 1:2). He knew the elect even before the earth was created! (Jeremiah 1:5; Ephesians 1:4) He knew us before we were born!

But with the precious blood of Christ, as of a lamb without blemish and without spot: 20Who verily was foreordained before the foundation of the world, but was manifest in these last times for you. (1 Peter 1:19:20)

Why? Why was the Lord "foreordained" to be our savior even before the "foundations of the world"? If sin had not already taken place before this [current] universal creation, then why did He predestine a plan for Himself to shed His own blood for the sins of many (Hebrews 9:28)?

Could it be, God was aware of sin even before "Adam" ever stepped foot on planet earth?

[God] knows every detail of the original sin and how each one of us would react to His plan of salvation. How does God know this? Because it already happened! Even so, the Lord our God placed upon Himself the burden of entering into this flesh to die as a righteous sacrifice so that all who accept His free gift of mercy (the womb/matrix) may believe in Him, repent, become partakers of His will in our lives, and one day "return to paradise." **[38]**

Foreknowledge fits predestination like a glove. Foreknowledge is not to suggest God can see future events that have not yet occurred. It is to suggest these events have already occurred. We are only now living out those events here on this side of the matrix, in this current physical realm.

Have you ever experienced déjà vu? Weird, right? The feeling is that you've been here before or that you are playing out a scenario that was intended to happen before it happened. Well, perhaps you have. And if so, it was a similar event that happened in a different realm, a realm that was not "physical" in the way we interpret physics here and now.

Since we know God is love personified in perfection, there can be no evil in Him. His righteousness and justice will inevitably result in getting rid of evil. This *riddance* of evil would appear to the faithless person as a *creation* of evil. But in fact, His decisions are righteous and just. Yes, God is *aware* of evil, and He knows that evil exists (Genesis 3:22), but that does not mean He is the *source* of that evil. It would be impossible for pure love to produce evil in the first place. Using harsh punishment (which appears to us mortals as an "evil force") is only used to *eliminate* evil as a result of God's justice which is *opposed* to evil. The mere thought of intentionally creating evil would be foreign to pure love. It is a contradiction in terms to suggest evil originated from love. The thought of "evil" being intentionally created by Himself would have never crossed God's "mind" during His original creation of Eden. His intentions would have been pure and loving. Once Satan came on the scene, God would have then known and experienced evil perverting His creation for the first time. God Himself did not pervert our creation, Satan did. At which point, He would have said, *"Adam… don't eat from that 'tree' over there. Do you understand me? It is bad for you. It will kill you."* Once "Adam" did indeed eat from that "tree," God saw fit to predestine a sacrificial plan of salvation for His fallen creatures.

God would recreate the universe (Genesis 1:2) with a promise to die for His creation whom He loves very much (John 3:16) and one day create a new heaven and new earth (Isaiah 65:17; 2 Peter 3:13; Revelation 21:1). Evil will be forever banished once and for all (Revelation 20:10). This time, Satan will be unable to enter the new heaven and new earth (Revelation 21:27) the way he had in God's original creation in "the Garden of Eden." Love will once again be free to live in harmony without outside interference (Revelation 22).

CHAPTER 6

The Origin of Free Will

The final item we need to address is free will. The thinking behind this is very similar to all other false assumptions mentioned thus far. It is commonly said that if God gave us free will, He would have known (because He presumably has foreknowledge) that free will would inevitably lead to sin and sin would lead to evil. Therefore, God is the root cause of evil and suffering. Hence, the false assumption that God intentionally created something He foreknew would be evil—free will.

Once again, are we not only assuming God gave us free will? Did God say, *Hey Adam, I would like you to tend to this garden. Go ahead and do whatever you think is best.* That type of "free will" is not even remotely close to what God commanded of Adam. God quite clearly commanded Adam to obey Him.

> And the LORD God commanded the man, saying, Of every tree of the garden thou mayest freely eat: [17]But of the tree of the knowledge of good and evil, thou shalt not eat of it: for in the day that thou eatest thereof thou shalt surely die. (Genesis 2:16–17)

He told Adam very specifically what He *was* allowed to do and what he *was not* allowed to do. Call me crazy, but that does not sound much like free will at all. That sounds like a very stern commandment! Do not "eat" from this one very specific "tree" or you will die!

Due to this understanding, a skeptic will make the argument that God is a self-righteous dictator. God forces us to do what He desires and punishes us when we do not do as He commands. In other words, God is a "malevolent bully" because He gave us "free will" only to punish us for exercising that free will. On the other hand, if we were to suggest God did *not* give us free will, the same skeptics would once again claim God is a dictator for not allowing us to make our own decisions. Whether the ability to exercise free will was granted by God or not, God is still a despot in their minds.

If a father commands his son not to touch the flame and the young boy does as he was told not to do, does that make the father a tyrant when the child gets burned?

If a father commands his daughter to never drink anything found under the sink because it is poisonous, does that make the father a dictator when she ends up in the hospital getting her stomach pumped?

God commands us to not do what He knows will kill us. God doesn't have to know what Satan's plans are, He just knows Satan is a liar and wants to destroy us. If that makes God a dictator, so be it. He is a dictator for our own good. He is a dictator for love and eternal life. God created a loving bond with His creation and then commanded them to stay away from "the serpent" who is trying to deceive them into believing a lie resulting in their deaths. How does that make Jehovah a bad father?

God created perfect love and harmony. This is known to some as "restricted free will" [39], meaning God would allow us "free will" but only to the extent that we choose between options that are pleasing to Him, which essentially *is* the case in the Garden of Eden. We are allowed to make decisions for ourselves with one stipulation. *Do not* decide to eat *that* "tree" or you will die. *That* is *not* "free will." That, if anything, is a *restricted* free will. Do anything you want, as long as you don't do "that."

Soon to follow the original creation in Eden, Satan trespassed and began destroying God's paradise by planting seeds of doubt (Genesis 3:4), seeds of deception (Genesis 3:5), and literally seeds of his own forbidden offspring of which he was certainly not permitted to do (Genesis 3:15; 6:4).

After Satan did what he did, God for the first time would have begun thinking of a way to "save that which is lost" (Luke 19:10). He then predestined a universal plan to recreate our existence for the sole purpose of allowing a likeness of Himself, His own begotten son, to be born into the flesh, live a sinless life, and then sacrifice His innocence as an atonement for the sins of His mortal children. God allowed His own son to be murdered by the same evil liar who started this whole mess in the first place. He did this to not only redeem the sinners and remove their sin but to prove His power and sovereign authority over the grave. It is only *He* who can destroy sin and death (Revelation 1:18; 20:14). And now, anybody who is willing to follow Jesus' commandments to love God and love one another can and will eventually return to paradise.

If Satan had never broken the rules of God's realm by deceiving "Eve," sin would never have entered creation. Mankind could have lived in paradise for an eternity without pain or suffering. The capacity to sin, which leads to evil, was never present in Eden, that is, not until "the dragon, that old serpent, which is the Devil and Satan" started working his eternal black magic known as *deception*.

Notice how in the end of Revelation, there is no sin in paradise, which means the ability to sin has been removed. The capacity to sin no longer exists. We will once again have a "restricted" free will. The one who created sin and evil will be banished from Eden (paradise) never to return. Satan will exist in an entirely separate eternal realm created specifically for him (Matthew 25:41). This realm is known as Geenna, outer darkness. This realm will not be in the same realm as Eden. They are two completely different dimensions. By removing Satan, God has removed the ability for His creatures to disobey Him and make a wrong decision. That is not "free will" any more than it is an absence of death. It is eternal life in bliss, the inability to make a wrong decision. Again, how does that make Jehovah a bad father? Is that not also the environment we wish to have for our own children?

Imagine if Satan had never entered the picture. Imagine if Satan never showed up in Jehovah's realm. That would mean Jehovah would have no need to command Adam to not eat from *that* specific "tree." If that "tree" had never shown up in Eden, God could have said, *Okay Adam, do whatever you want. Nothing here can harm you.* That would mean "free will" (the ability to choose between right and wrong) would be irrelevant. Adam can do whatever he chooses because there is literally no possibility of making a mistake.

The capacity to sin was present in the original creation as a result of Satan's trespass. Thank God Almighty; Satan will *not* be present in the universe of tomorrow.

~

There is another sense of free will that rarely gets the attention it deserves. Consider what it is to be sovereign over your own creation. If you are the only sovereign creator in your realm, that means you and only you have the authority to change your creation to how you see fit, which means that, in turn, you are the only one with "free will." *Your* creation does not have free will. *Your* creation cannot change what *you* have created (adding evil where it does not belong). But if someone else from another realm enters into your realm who also has the ability to create, that person can now start meddling with *your* creation, in turn, giving *your* creation a "choice" between *you* and "something else" for the first time. At *that* point…your creation would now have free will.

Imagine now that you have created a beautiful clay pot. Imagine also that you have an adversary who hates you very much. You cannot understand why he hates you so much. You're not sure what he is thinking, only that your desire is for him to stop doing what he is doing and just leave you alone. At some point when you were not looking, this adversary swooped in and knocked your beautiful clay pot off the shelf. You return to find the broken pieces of your beautiful pot strewn about the floor.

The *clay pot* did *not* have free will. This pot was only a pot; it didn't know any better. It was tipped over by an outside force—the adversary. This is where free will comes into play. This pot cannot fix itself. Only its creator can recreate the pot and choose to put the pieces back together.

Now, this creator could have very well used His free will to sweep up the broken pieces and toss them in the trash. But what did He do? Jehovah used *His* free will to recreate the pot by offering it new life in a different existence. However, in order to enter into this new existence, the clay pieces would need to be remolded once again and hardened by the flame.

This life, this creation, this universe is that flame. *Jesus* is that flame which remolds us into something new. The definition of this name "Jesus" (H3091; *yᵊhôšûaʿ*; G2424; *iēsous*) in its original Hebrew form literally means "Jehovah Saves."

Jehovah could have used His free will to say, *Nope, they betrayed me and followed a criminal who perverted my creation, and they have now become criminals themselves. They curse my name and hate me for creating them. I will send them all to hell's fire to show those evil creatures who's in charge of this realm.*

That of course would be assuming Jehovah is evil when, in fact, we know Jehovah is pure love!

He could have cast us aside like a broken vessel, but He chose to use His free will and sovereignty to put us all back together!

Jehovah chose to enter into His own broken creation to sacrifice Himself publicly for the whole world to see so that for all time, people would know how much He truly loves us. Think about that for five minutes… even after we betrayed Him, He was still willing to die for us.

This is the fourth of "four solutions" mentioned in the introduction.

God did not create free will. He created perfection. If anything, He created a "restricted free will," which in its definition is not free will at all! So-called free will was created at the moment Satan introduced the concept of "an alternative" to "Eve." Satan twisted God's perfect creation by introducing the concept of doubt. It is only at *that* moment that God's creatures (both man and angel) were presented with "a choice." If it were not for this "choice," they would have never "chosen" to "eat" the "fruit." It is only at *that* moment of choice that God's creatures were presented with the opportunity of *un*restricted "free will" — the ability to distinguish between right and wrong, good and evil. If it were not for Satan's outside influence, this existence we are now living never would have been created. We would still be in Eden. Satan created the option for "free will," not Jehovah!

In a perfect state of existence, there is no need to choose between "right and wrong" or "good and evil" because "wrong" and "evil" do not exist!

> Now Paradisal man always chose to follow God's will. In following it he also gratified his own desire, both because all the actions demanded of him were, in fact, agreeable to his blameless inclination, and also because the service of God was itself his keenest pleasure, without which as their razor edge all joys would have been insipid to him.
> …If the thing we like doing is, in fact, the thing God wants us to do, yet that is not our reason for doing it; it remains a mere happy coincidence. **[40]**

And therefore, the will of God is perfectly endowed in all His creatures. The will of God supersedes "free will." "Free will" implies God's will is not necessary, or that it is not at the forefront of our desires at all times.

Who needs the ideology of "free will" when there are no possibilities to make a bad decision? And why are there no possibilities to make a bad decision? Because sin has been removed from creation! Just as it was in the Garden of Eden before Satan began planting his "seeds."

Who needs the ideology of "free will" when there is nothing poisonous to choose from? And why is there nothing poisonous to choose from? Because the poisonous "tree" has been cut down by the roots and thrown into the fire!

Evil, and therefore the capacity to make a wrong decision, does not exist. There is no capacity to make a wrong decision. Hence, the "free will" argument is an irrelevant paradox.

How can we have "free will" when the will of God is the only thing on our mind? How can we have "free will" when the will of God is the only will in existence?

Thank God Almighty for His perfect and loving will. Amen.

CHAPTER 7

Additional Considerations

When Christ was questioned by the religious leaders about why He spent time with sinners, He responded by stating it is not the healthy who need a doctor, but the sick (Mark 2:17). As a devout thinker and philosopher in his own right, C.S. Lewis' insight often cut through these topics with razor-sharp precision.

> Prostitutes are in no danger of finding their present life so satisfactory that they cannot turn to God: the proud, the avaricious, the self-righteous, are in that danger. [41]

In this case, a depressed, loveless prostitute would ask, why? *Why was I born into this life, God? Why can I not find a way out of this? Why do you allow this to happen?* In longing for understanding and hope for a better future, this person would turn to God for help. No doubt, just like Mary Magdalene, God would receive this woman with open arms, love, and forgiveness. God's love for His children is so overwhelming that we likely have no way in our mortal understanding to truly comprehend its full reach.

Now, some would strike back at such a loving claim with Old Testament scriptures asking *why* God commanded the death of so many people.

How do we reconcile the God of the Old Testament with the God of the New Testament? Again, this is a misleading question. We need to put things in the proper perspective.

To start, we should point out the fact that Jesus is not all together the pacifist type commune leader that a lot of people make Him out to be. Yes, He asks us to forgive our enemies and "turn the other cheek" to those who would strike us. But He also authored a dire warning of pain and suffering that He is going to personally rain down upon the human race. Some of the things Jesus said are not at all a fun-loving type forgive-and-forget theodicy. In fact, some of what Jesus taught is, dare we say, identical to that of the Old Testament punishments, even much worse in some cases.

> Woe unto thee, Chorazin! woe unto thee, Bethsaida! for if the mighty works, which were done in you, had been done in Tyre and Sidon, they would have repented long ago in sackcloth and ashes. [22]But I say unto you, It shall be more tolerable for Tyre and Sidon at the day of judgment, than for you. [23]And thou, Capernaum, which art exalted unto heaven, shalt be brought down to hell: for if the mighty works, which have been done in thee, had been done in Sodom, it would have remained until this day. [24]But I say unto you, That *it shall be more tolerable for the land of Sodom in the day of judgment, than for thee.* (Matthew 11:21–24)

On one of His ministerial journeys, Christ told the people of Chorazin and Bethsaida that their punishment was going to be worse than that of Tyre, Sidon, Sodom, and Gomorrah. We know the cities of Tyre and Sidon were destroyed by Nebuchadnezzar and once again by Alexander the Great but also the Judgments given by God's prophecies (Isaiah 23; Jeremiah 25; 27; 47; Ezekiel 26–28; Joel 3; Amos 1; Zachariah 9). Among other sins, their worshiping of false gods was their downfall.

Sodom and Gomorrah of course were so perverse in their dealings with one another that God saw fit to destroy their cities with fire. So in this case alone, and for all who refuse to repent before the day of judgment, Christ is *not* "turning the other check" by any means. He is most assuredly the same God of the Old Testament.

So let us put this into context and not confuse Jesus with a lesser version of His perfect and righteous wrath.

> As therefore the tares are gathered and burned in the fire; so shall it be in the end of this world. [41]The Son of man shall send forth his angels, and they shall gather out of his kingdom all things that offend, and them which do iniquity; [42]And shall cast them into a furnace of fire: there shall be wailing and gnashing of teeth. (Matthew 13:40–42)

> For then shall be great tribulation, such as was not since the beginning of the world to this time, no, nor ever shall be. [22]And except those days should be shortened, there should no flesh be saved: but for the elect's sake those days shall be shortened. (Matthew 24:21–22)

And I saw heaven opened, and behold a white horse; and
he that sat upon him was called Faithful and True, and in
righteousness *he doth judge and make war.* ¹²His eyes were
as a flame of fire, and on his head were many crowns; and
he had a name written, that no man knew, but he himself.
¹³And *he was clothed with a vesture dipped in blood*: and his
name is called The Word of God. ¹⁴And the armies which
were in heaven followed him upon white horses, clothed
in fine linen, white and clean. ¹⁵And out of his mouth goeth
a sharp sword, that with it *he should smite the nations*: and he
shall rule them with a rod of iron: and *he treadeth the wine-
press of the fierceness and wrath of Almighty God.* (Revelation
19:11–15)

That does not sound like pacifism, nor does it sound like
the hippy-dippy free-loving God we all portray Jesus to be.
In fact, it sounds exactly like the very stern and relentless
wrath of God in the Old Testament!

As overflowing with love as Jesus truly is, He is still a
God that cannot and will not tolerate sin to enter His kingdom (Genesis 3:23–24).

Since this is the case, why do we say these two Gods
(Old and New Testaments) have two different views on
punishment? Why do we say one is harsh and the other is
all-forgiving? No, in all God's *love* and all His perfect and
righteous judgment, these "two Gods" are no less than
identical!

This is a warning to all mankind. The wrath of God is
not to be trifled with. Yes, Christ commands us to love one
another. Unfortunately, there is no other choice than to issue
justice for evil deeds. And so Satan, his angels, and all the

souls among mankind who knowingly and willingly chose to follow Satan's treachery must therefore be punished.

The reason God commanded *us* to be loving and virtuous is because that is the way it was in the Garden of Eden, and that is the way it will be in the new heavens and new earth! We are practicing *now* for how to love in a future scenario when we will return to His kingdom!

> Do not repay anyone evil for evil. Be careful to do what is right in the eyes of everyone. [18]If it is possible, as far as it depends on you, live at peace with everyone. [19]Do not take revenge, my dear friends, but leave room for God's wrath, for it is written: "It is mine to avenge; I will repay," says the Lord. [20]On the contrary: "If your enemy is hungry, feed him; if he is thirsty, give him something to drink. In doing this, you will heap burning coals on his head." [21]Do not be overcome by evil, but overcome evil with good."(Romans 12:17–21; NIV)

Those who practice love in this life will enter into paradise after all prophecies have come to pass. Those who choose to practice evil will be destroyed by God... forever.

~

Let's talk about this Old Testament God. *Why* were the people of the earth so bad that God needed to destroy the whole earth with a flood? Why would He kill all humans on earth and only save eight people? Again, we need to put this all into perspective. It needs to be understood in context. To do so, we should offer this one obvious question.

Are the people God destroyed in the flood *His* human creations?

If you answered yes to this question, you would be wrong. God did not kill a bunch of people simply because they would not worship Him. He destroyed them because they were literally angel-human hybrids. "Aliens" (literally) came down to earth from up in the sky and began mating with the "daughters of men." You think those UFOs are little gray men from Mars? Nope, they are angels and demons, physical, just like us.

> That the sons of God saw the daughters of men that they were fair; and they took them wives of all which they chose. [3]And the LORD said, My spirit shall not always strive with man, for that *he also is flesh*: yet his days shall be an hundred and twenty years. [4]There were giants in the earth in those days; and also after that, when the sons of God came in unto the daughters of men, and they bare children to them, the same became mighty men which were of old, men of renown. (Genesis 6:2–4)

What does it mean to say that "he" (referring to woman as "mankind") is "*also* flesh"?

What does it mean that we are created in the image of Elohim? (Genesis 1:26)

What does it mean that the angels who visited Abraham literally looked just like humans?

The answer is quite simple: it means the angels have flesh bodies just like us. That is what the Bible says. These angels even sat down and had a meal with Abraham (Genesis 18).

This is not a joke. Satan convinced the angels, the "sons of Elohim," to do what they were not permitted to do, to create angel-human hybrids by mating with the mortals of mankind. The earth became so polluted with these hybrid humans that eventually all flesh had been corrupted, that is, except for Noah and his family who were likely the only purebred humans remaining who were also still worshiping their rightful Loving Creator.

> These are the generations of Noah: Noah was a just man and *perfect* in his *generations*, and Noah walked with God. 10And Noah begat three sons, Shem, Ham, and Japheth. (Genesis 6:9)

This word "generations" (H8435; *tôwlᵉdâh*) means "his decent," his history, his family. *Towldah* is referring to his own personal heritage, his family tree. So, what would it mean to suggest his "family tree" was perfect, that is, without spot or blemish? Clearly, it is because Noah's family had not taken part in Satan's rebellious inbreeding in Genesis 3:15 and Genesis 6.

It could not be more obvious. This "flesh" of both angels and mankind is a result of God's "seed" and Satan's "seed" in the Garden of Eden parable.

God did not destroy His own creation, per se. God destroyed a rebellious forbidden offspring and all their human sex companions because their thoughts were "only evil continually" (Genesis 6:5).

A similar sentiment can be said for all the other times in the Old Testament where the LORD God commanded Israel to perform what atheists now refer to as "genocide." These people were predestined to evil and damnation because the Lord already knew the desires of their heart. He knew they had absolutely no desire to repent, not even if they had eternal life — they would seek with all their being to dethrone the father of forgiveness. They hate God. They hate His sovereignty. And they hate the idea that God commands them to be good and loving.

~

When addressing the problem of evil, believers are inevitably confronted with the book of Job. A person can ask how in the world a loving God could have allowed such terrible circumstances to befall an innocent man like Job.

Remember, by this time in creation (Job 1–2), God is already aware of Satan's treacheries in the Garden of Eden. The sins in Eden had already, or were currently, taking place. In fact, there is evidence to suggest the book of Job is a direct reference to the Garden of Eden. That is to say, the story of Job literally took place in Eden, not our current planet earth. Job lived "in the east" (Job 1:2) which is a direct reference to the Garden of Eden parable (Genesis 2:8)

> Now the Lord God had planted *a garden in the east*, in Eden; and there he put the man he had formed. (Genesis 2:8; NIV)

> He was the greatest man among all *the people of the East*. (Job 1:2; NIV)

It could very well be that by God's allowance of giving Satan free reign in Job's life, God was proving a point of how resentful, hateful, and treacherous Satan truly is. By allowing this scenario to play out without God's interference (Satan's free will), Satan was ensuring his own demise. Satan's judgment would be established for all God's creation to see with their own eyes. By standing back and allowing Satan to express *his* free will, God has proven that Satan's actions are worthy of eternal punishment.

God had nothing to do with what happened to Job, but He will have everything to do with what happens to Satan. The perpetrator is the man who seals his own fate.

The saga of Job's torment was a way God could prove to all His creatures that Satan did in fact deserve the future punishment predestined for him. It is the same for all pain and suffering throughout history. By the time Job's torment had begun, God had already created Satan's prison—hell. The guilty verdict had already been assigned in his trial, but the sentence had yet to be carried out.

Imagine if a person on trial stood up and attacked the prosecuting attorney right there in front of the entire courtroom. He would be proving firsthand to all who were present that he was indeed capable of the crime and guilty of the charges brought against him. The defendant would have "shown his true colors" by acting out in the courtroom.

This life, this planetary existence we are now living, this is Satan's trial. By God allowing Satan to have free will over God's creation (to cause evil, pain, and suffering), God is showing the whole world that Satan is indeed worthy of eternal punishment. And just like Job, God will then restore those whom Satan has tortured with his evil presence.

> After Job had prayed for his friends, the Lord restored his fortunes and gave him twice as much as he had before. (Job 42:10; NIV)

Satan will soon be thrown into prison with a "lifetime sentence" where no bond or bail will ever be allowed. And since Satan is a creature existing from eternity, his "life sentence" is eternal separation from God in a prison built specifically for him and all those who knowingly and willingly followed his deceptive ways.

God would not have known what Satan was planning on doing to Job, only that He knew Satan was going to prove to the judge and jury that he is guilty of his crimes! Thus, justifying the prosecutions plan to throw Satan in prison—forever.

You see, God did not *want* Satan to do what he did or enjoy the concept of Satan's evil free will. However, God did *allow* Satan (and all his evil ways) to run its full course. This proved at least two things that God can now bring forward on judgment day.

First, Satan is unrepentant. His verdict of guilty is justified. God is forgiving to the repentant, but He is also just to the evildoers. He has given Satan every opportunity to stop doing what he is doing. When Satan's sentence is carried out, God's judgment will have been fair, righteous, and 100% transparent.

Second, Satan's "free will" is what gets people into so much trouble. If we (those persecuted by Satan's evil free will) stay loyal to Jehovah the way Job stayed loyal during persecution, we will all one day be restored in the same way Job was restored (Job 42:10). But if we choose to knowingly and willingly make people suffer the way Satan made Job to suffer, we are going to inherit the same judgment given to Satan.

God knew He was going to restore Job to a state of health and happiness even before Job had undergone such heartache under Satan's persecution.

God allowed Satan to torment Job knowing full well the outcome was a guilty verdict for Satan and an innocent verdict for Job combined with more reparations than Job had ever considered.

Thus, God's judgment is proven to be righteous. When God allowed Satan to treat Job so poorly, He was proving Satan could have, if he chose to, treated job with love. Allowing this scenario to play out was the only way of proving Satan's sentence of eternal punishment is justifiable. God is not going to send a person to "hell's fire" unless they knowingly and willingly choose that same fate.

~

> One day the sons of God came to present themselves before the LORD, and Satan also came with them. (Job 1:6)

Why does the Bible consistently differentiate between the sons of God, and Satan?

Why was Satan "also" with the sons of God?

If Satan was created by God, why is he not also called a "son of God"?

The Lord said to Satan, *"Where have **you** come from?"* (Job 1:7; NIV)

If Satan is one of God's creations, how exactly would the omnipresent foreknowing creator God not know that Satan had been down walking throughout *His* creation?

Satan answered the Lord, "From roaming throughout the earth, going back and forth on it." 8Then the Lord said to Satan, "Have you considered my servant Job? There is no one on earth like him; he is blameless and upright, a man who fears God and shuns evil." (Job 1:7–8; NIV)

Satan just admitted to God, "I was down walking in your creation, what is it to you?" The final point to make is this: not here in the book of Job nor anywhere else in the Bible does it ever say Satan is one of God's creations. Therefore, if Satan is *not* one of God's creations, then Jehovah is *not* the *Evil God of Love* we all portray Him to be.

~

In the introduction to this book, I proposed a very common question:

If the God of the Old Testament is the same God of the New Testament, how do we explain the clear discrepancies in His teachings?

...why does He Himself perform such evil atrocities according to His own written testament?" (Genesis 6–8; Genesis 18–19; Exodus 11–12; Leviticus 18:24–25; Numbers 21:2–3; Deuteronomy 9:3; 20:17; Joshua 6:17, 21; 1 Samuel 15)

"Is God a hypocrite?"

Why did God command the deaths of entire nations of people such as the stories told in the Old Testament?

This should be very simple to understand if we remove our bias and think about this logically and in light of all the evidence presented in the DoctrineParadox.com book series.

The Israelites were predestined to be the bloodline that would usher in the Messiah and, therefore, God's personal salvation offered to a fallen race. This Messiah would be God in the flesh who takes away the sins of the world. He would enter into His own fallen creation for the sole purpose of putting His love on display for all the world to see. He would allow His own self-existence to be executed in a more gruesome manner than any of the punishments dealt out in the Old Testament. Sodom and Gomorrah was most likely a rather quick death, not as agonizing as being tortured and nailed to a cross for several hours, not as quick or sufficient as the business end of a sword. No, God willingly chose to be executed at that specific time and place in that specific manner to show how patient He truly is. But more importantly, He did it to show the world's inhabitants the sign of Jonah, three days and three nights in the belly of the earth.

His dead and lifeless body was resurrected from hades by the power of our Living God in Heaven. Jesus would then show Himself alive to many people proving He is who He claimed to be—the author of eternal life in paradise.

The reason these other tribes of people had to die is that they had already made their choice to follow Satan and all his rebellious ways. They knew the miracles of God and had even witnessed some of them personally throughout the years, and yet, they did not care. They were not willing to follow Jehovah because Jehovah asks them to repent and turn away from their sins. For them, that is asking too much. They love their sins more than they love the prospect of following Jehovah's rules. They hope to one day overthrow Jehovah's reign and take Him off His throne (Isaiah 14).

So, to make way for the Messiah, God took these rebellious people out of the picture. He killed those who were already spiritually dead and unwilling to repent. And how did He know they were unwilling to repent? Because He knew them before they were born!

If these lost souls possessed any desire to love God and love one another, they would not have been destroyed in that manner.

It truly is that simple. This is God's creation. If we do not follow God's rules (love God and love one another), we will not be permitted to stay in His Kingdom. How is that too difficult to understand?

~

Imagine this scenario. A man you know to be vile and cruel shows up to your house, invites himself in, makes himself a meal, and then wonders into your daughter's bedroom and slams the door behind him while shouting back at you, "Mind your own business!"

As a father who loves his daughter very much, what would you do? Would you say, *"To hell with my daughter. How dare she not come out of that bedroom."* As outrageous as this scenario sounds, it is in fact similar to the treacheries committed by Satan and his rebellious offspring. And yet, in this scenario, the daughter did in fact willingly have an affair with this disgraceful intruder. Satan's treacheries have led our Loving Creator God to pain and heartbreak (Genesis 6:6).

Do we really possess the audacity to question the motives of this loving father?

Who are we to suggest this brokenhearted man should *not* offer the two of them a good old-fashioned butt whopping?

What do workers gain from their toil? [10]I have seen the burden God has laid on the human race. [11]He has made everything beautiful in its time. *He has also set eternity in the human heart; yet no one can fathom what God has done from beginning to end.* [12]I know that there is nothing better for people than to be happy and to do good while they live. [13]That each of them may eat and drink, and find satisfaction in all their toil—this is the gift of God. [14]I know that everything God does will endure forever; nothing can be added to it and nothing taken from it. *God does it so that people will fear him.* (Ecclesiastes 3:9–14; NIV)

The idea behind survival of the fittest tells us that we should possess a healthy dose of self-preservation if we are to survive this evolutionary process. And yet, if we had even the smallest inkling of self-preservation, we would fear our Loving Creator God and do as He commands.

> Whoever corrects a mocker invites insults; whoever rebukes the wicked incurs abuse. [8]Do not rebuke mockers or they will hate you; rebuke the wise and they will love you. [9]Instruct the wise and they will be wiser still; teach the righteous and they will add to their learning. [10]*The fear of the Lord is the beginning of wisdom, and knowledge of the Holy One is understanding.* [11]For through wisdom your days will be many, and years will be added to your life. [12]If you are wise, your wisdom will reward you; if you are a mocker, you alone will suffer. (Proverbs 9:7–12)

Name one decent and honest father who does not discipline his children when they step out of line? Only a poor and selfish father would allow his children to continue wayward without rebuking them. A good father will punish his children's disobedience and then spend years explaining why punishment was necessary. Unless that pestilent child willingly becomes the fool they portray, to become aware of their own sinful condition, they will never understand the love of their father.

> Let no man deceive himself. If any man among you seemeth to be wise in this world, let him become a fool, that he may be wise. [19]For the wisdom of this world is foolishness with God. For it is written, He taketh the wise in their own craftiness. [20]And again, The Lord knoweth the thoughts of the wise, that they are vain. (1 Corinthians 3:18–20)

So, why does evil exist? It exists because an eternal creature known as Satan entered into God's Garden of Eden with the intention of turning God's creation against their creator. God never knew the full extent of what Satan had planned.

Evil is not a thing. It is an action, a result of Satan's contradiction to God's will, which was illegally foisted upon Jehovah's creation without His foreknowledge.

The reason good and innocent people like Job suffer through pain and heartache is because Satan *willed* it to be so. Not Jehovah.

Why did God *create* evil? He didn't. He created perfect love in perfect harmony. Satan created the potential for evil by doing what he knew he was never permitted to do.

Why did God *create* free will? He didn't. He created paradise without the possibility of sin or death. It was us, God's creation, that turned away from Him and sought other gods only *after* paradise had been manipulated by an outside force.

Why does God *allow* evil? He allows it for at least three reasons.

First, to prove how patient and loving He truly is.

Second, to make know to His creation how He gave every single one of His children every possible chance, even on multiple occasions, the opportunity to *repent* and begin practicing love.

Third, God allows evil because He wants us all to understand this pain and suffering is the result of following Satan. This word "Satan" (H7854; *sâṭân*) literally means "opponent" or "adversary." The root word (H7853; *sâtan*) means "to attack."

The definition of the name of Satan is "the adversary attacks."

God allows suffering because He needs us to know how good we could have had it in Eden if we were to never have listened to Satan. God wants us to know we are able to escape the pain and suffering of this current existence by adhering to the teachings of His Son, Jesus; meaning literally, "Jehovah Saves."

The name of Satan means literally "the adversary attacks", whereas the name of Jesus means literally, "Jehovah saves." How could this possibly be a coincidence?

Why do "good people" experience pain and suffering? For the same reason our children must "suffer" when they disobey, get in trouble with the authorities, and require a just discipline for their actions. Every single person to enter into the flesh is here for one reason. We broke the law—God's law. This life is the opportunity to repent and ask forgiveness for our crimes.

> If we say that we have no sin, we deceive ourselves, and the truth is not in us. ⁹If we confess our sins, he is faithful and just to forgive us our sins, and to cleanse us from all unrighteousness. (1 John 1: 8–9)

If God has sovereignty over His broken creation, why does He not come down here and fix this mess Himself?

He did. That was Jesus' sole mission. Moreover, He will return some day to take us back into His Kingdom. He will punish those who knowingly and willingly led others astray and He will forgive those who willingly choose to seek a loving existence in His presence.

The skeptics insist Christians have been backed into an impossible corner when it comes to addressing the problem of evil or the possibility of an omnipotent loving creator. They could not be farther from the truth.

As the evidence in this book illustrates, it is they who have an impossible task of proving "morality" is only a figment of our imagination.

It is they who have the burden of proving "survival of the fittest" can in any way produce the capacity for Love.

It is they who have the impossible task of proving the nonexistence of God.

It is they who have the blinders of false science covering their eyes.

Ultimately it is *we* the believers who have the upper hand by placing our faith in Christ — our Loving Creator God, the King of Kings and Lord of Lords.

May you never stop seeking the truth in the gospel of His everlasting word. Praise be to God in the highest. Amen!

Endnotes

[1] C.S. Lewis, *The Problem of Pain* (New York: Macmillan, 1944), 91

[2] https://doctrineparadox.com/2019/05/08/what-is-the-matrix/

[3] https://www.youtube.com/watch?v=SwifX03d9QU

[4] Richard Dawkins, *The God Delusion* (Boston: Houghton Mifflin 2006), 31.

[5] Philip Walls, *The Christian Doctrine Paradox* (Genesis Publishing House, 2022), ix-xiv.

[6] Dante Alighieri, *Inferno III* (public domain)

[7] Charles Mathewes, Ph.D., *Why Evil Exists* (Chantilly: The Great Courses, 2011), 194

[8] Ibid., 238

[9] Ibid., 268

[10] Josh McDowell, *The New Evidence that Demands a Verdict* (Nashville: Thomas Nelson 1999).

[11] Peter Kreeft, Fundamentals of the Faith (San Francisco: Ignatius Press, 1988)

[12] Ibid., 54

[13] Ibid., 56

[14] Greg Welty, *Why Is There Evil In The World (And So Much Of It)?* (Scotland: Christian Focus Publications Ltd, 2018)

[15] Ibid., 12-13

[16] Ibid., 15

[17] Paul Copan, *Is God a Moral Monster?* (Grand Rapids: Baker Books, 2011), 11

[18] Gerry Burney, *Science Origins and Ancient Civilization* (Xulon Press: 2014); https://targettruthministries.com/

[19] Kent Hovind, Creation Seminar Series, https://shop.drdino.com/collections/all-dvds/products/copy-of-css-complete-set-dr-hovinds-award-winning-creation-seminar-series

[20] Ken Ham, https://www.youtube.com/channel/UCOtgG1fKGni_YHapU4RMMRQ

[21] https://answersingenesis.org/; https://www.youtube.com/@answersingenesis

[22] Creation Museum, https://creationmuseum.org/creation-science/

[23] Philip Walls, *The Christian Doctrine Paradox* (Genesis Publishing House, 2022), 220-278

[24] Ibid., 224-225

[25] Ibid., 222-223

[26] Ibid., 281-282

[27] Ibid., 250

[28] https://www.youtube.com/watch?v=SwifX03d9QU

[29] Philip Walls, *The Christian Doctrine Paradox* (Genesis Publishing House, 2022), 237-240

[30] https://www.blueletterbible.org/lexicon/h5175/kjv/wlc/0-1/

[31] Unless otherwise noted, all Hebrew and Greek definitions were taken from: Strong, James, *The New Strong's Expanded Exhaustive Concordance of the Bible* (Thomas Nelson, 2010), H2416,

[32] Unless otherwise noted, all Hebrew and Greek definitions were taken from: Strong, James, *The New Strong's Expanded Exhaustive Concordance of the Bible* (Thomas Nelson, 2010), H430

[33] Philip Walls, *The Christian Doctrine Paradox* (Genesis Publishing House, 2022), 240

[34] Ibid., 225-276

[35] Unless otherwise noted, all Hebrew and Greek definitions were taken from: Strong, James, *The New Strong's Expanded Exhaustive Concordance of the Bible* (Thomas Nelson, 2010), G622

[36] NEW C.S. Lewis, The Problem of Pain (New York: Macmillan, 1944), 129

[37] https://doctrineparadox.com/2023/03/21/the-evil-god-of-love/

[38] Philip Walls, *The Christian Doctrine Paradox* (Genesis Publishing House, 2022), 247-248.

[39] Greg Welty, Why Is There Evil In The World (And So Much Of It)? (Scotland: Christian Focus Publications Ltd, 2018), 160-162

[40] C.S. Lewis, The Problem of Pain (New York: Macmillan, 1944), 97

[41] Ibid., 96